LIBRAS DON'T SAY NO

Also by Rosie Swale

Rosie Darling
Children of Cape Horn

ROSIE SWALE

LIBRAS DON'T SAY NO

PAUL ELEK
GRANADA PUBLISHING
London Toronto Sydney New York

Granada Publishing Limited
Frogmore, St Albans, Herts AL2 2NF
and

3 Upper James Street, London W1R 4BP
866 United Nations Plaza, New York, NY 10017, USA
117 York Street, Sydney, NSW 2000, Australia
100 Skyway Avenue, Rexdale, Ontario M9W 3A6, Canada
PO Box 84165, Greenside, 2034 Johannesburg, South Africa
CML Centre, Queen & Wyndham Streets, Auckland 1,
New Zealand

Published by Granada Publishing in Paul Elek Ltd 1980

ISBN 0 236 40172 6

Printed in Great Britain by
Richard Clay (The Chaucer Press) Ltd, Bungay, Suffolk

Contents

This book is dedicated to the bulldog 'Twopeople' Stonesteps Saffron, who put a spell on my life.

She went before it was published. But bulldogs never die. 'Twopeople' lives in this book; and the book through her.

Blessed be.

ONE

Thank the Goddess for Oxfam shops

'I'm sorry, Dr Simmons is out!'

The suave young man seemed lost in the vast marble reception room as he spoke.

'OH NO I'M NOT!' a voice boomed suddenly on the intercom. 'I saw the young lady arrive through the gates!'

The door shut behind me with a click as I walked in. A large man was sitting behind an ornate desk. He was completely naked. One of my books open at the photographs lay near the telephone.

'Come and sit on my knee,' he said. He reached out, knocking over the picture of his wife and children on his desk, grabbed me between the legs with no ceremony, and went on: 'On my first job syphoning oil in South America I got into trouble because there was always water in the oil. It turned out to be sweat off my own forehead. I may be a chairman now, but I'm still a wild person underneath – like you!'

'But, but – you must have lots of girlfriends,' I stammered, shades of my old hitch-hiking days coming back. 'You are such a fine-looking man. You don't need *me* ...!'

He glanced at the picture of the catamaran in my folder and shuddered.

'Let's not talk of boats now ... my darling ... I fell in love with you when I looked out of the window and saw you arrive. Those silver shoes ... It's all right my darling, the room is soundproof.'

This was the chairman of a large British corporation.

'Just please take your clothes off,' he whispered. 'I only want to see you.'

I tried to tell him that there are plenty of naked skins

in *The Sun* each day. But it didn't seem important, so I obliged.

He put on his spectacles. 'If you can come to me like this every week, I'll put £10,000 into your account to-morrow.'

I wrenched myself away from him. It was easy. He wasn't fit. I felt quite sorry for him. But for me the oldest profession in the world is sailing.

'NO THANK YOU,' I told him in the voice I sometimes used with our children Eve and Jimmy.

The siren that had been howling for the past two minutes got louder and more insistent. A harsh buzzer rang on his desk.

'I told you I was not to be disturbed!'

He listened and his face drooped and the grey under-coat of his skin showed through. He turned back towards me.

'There's a BOMB SCARE,' he whispered. 'They're evacuating the building.'

I didn't know whether to be pleased or sorry. The chairman pressed a button on his desk and the door unclicked its lock.

Hastily I clutched my fur coat around me. I glanced back once and saw the man stumbling clumsily into smart pin-striped trousers. I fled down through the vast corridors. It was not sponsorship I deserved, I thought, but danger money!

I reached the gates and from somewhere within the building I had just left came a loud bang. Had the IRA come to the rescue for once? I hoped the chairman hadn't been hurt. Maybe, I thought, I should have stayed and helped him.

It was quite cold now and my coat belt did up tighter than usual. All at once I realized that I had left all my clothes in the fat chairman's office! I had to get all the way from London to Southampton in time to tuck my children into their sleeping bags and kiss them goodnight. I really couldn't go all that way with no clothes on!

'40 gns' said the ticket on a sacklike dress in Harvey

Nichols. I shut my eyes, wrapped my coat round my knees more firmly and took the bus to Kensington. '40 pence' said the label on a similar dress in an Oxfam shop up Campden Hill.

'Excuse me please,' I asked the porter at the main entrance of the Royal Garden Hotel. His expression was respectful as my fine fake fur did my introductions.

'Has Lady Springbloom arrived yet?'

He shook his head and I hoped the name I'd just made up was really fictitious. 'Oh by the way – where is the ladies' powder room?'

Five minutes later I was at last dressed again. The ladies' loo attendant was looking at me a bit strangely. To distract her I gave her a paperback copy of my first book, *Rosie Darling*. It had been meant for the chairman.

The plush pink loo seemed a strange destination for a book written thousands of miles from land and whose godparents were the killer whales of the Pacific. It seemed a hundred lives ago since we had sailed into Plymouth after our 33,000-mile voyage to Australia and back round Cape Horn in our 30-foot catamaran *Anneliese*; light years since we had sighted the Lizard and Eve had shouted: 'Look, Mummy, look! There's an island called England!' We didn't know then that we'd be coming back to adventures that made Cape Horn seem a fair and gentle giant...

TWO

Had we changed? – or had the world changed?

... Eddystone Lighthouse blinked through a négligée of silken morning mist as we dunked the faithful washing-up bucket into the relentless cold seawater a last time and washed our hair. Afterwards the children's heads smelt of seaweed and the shore.

Suddenly we heard voices.

'You've left the radio on, silly girl!' Colin called.

Guiltily I stumbled down to see. But it stood quite silent. *Off* and off watch. Then there was a roar and a shout of engines and men ...

A launch full of beaming people came snorting noisily up to *Anneliese*'s seaweedy stern. The ocean spell was broken. The sky would be ours alone no longer. We had become selfish and greedy for them. But the beautiful sunsets wouldn't be only for us anymore. My knees trembled with fright. I held Colin's hand tightly, making steering difficult. It was ridiculous. These were friends.

The whole boat rocked as our literary agent leapt on board. The kiss he gave me startled me, and my Evo Stik repaired front crown wobbled. He was clutching a bottle; also a white and brown striped shirt for Colin and a bewildering parcel of garments for me.

Most of our clothes had broken the hearts of the clothes-pegs and flown away thousands of miles on ocean breezes long ago – lost except for the amusement of dolphins and seabeings. The veteran remains had mostly been divided as rags for the engines or nappies for baby Jimmy. The sea took care only of its own. Rust clogged trouser zips, which now hung entertainingly undone. Mould instead of feathers lined the sleeping bags. Each night for the last weeks we had tucked little Eve into 900 square foot of green, white and gold spinnaker instead.

Now two-year-old Jimmy, feet wedged securely against the swell, remained happily settled on the pink 'parson's potty' which the kindly parson in the Falkland Islands had given him, while Eve waved at the people as if they were a school of dolphins come to greet us.

Sausage rolls and sandwiches were passed over. Our stomachs rumbled and gurgled in dark panic for their familiar brown rice and Oxo cube diet. We looked curiously at leaves and sticks and bits of Colin's native country drifting around us.

Anneliese was quite happy. The water didn't taste any different to her hulls from that around Cape Horn, just a little warmer. But for us, coming in to land was now just as alarming as going out to sea had been when we had unleashed our muddy moorings in the River Itchen and first started sailing just three years ago.

We felt very proud of our little home. We gave *Anneliese* the chance to become the first catamaran round Cape Horn because we loved and trusted her. Now she'd achieved this while remaining a happy family home for us all; and she had brought us back to England safely too.

But a warning voice seemed to cry through the clamour clouding our senses: 'Go out to sea again,' it whispered. 'Stay away from the false gods ashore. Go back into the deep ocean, the 360 degrees of your familiar blue and white horizon home. The majestic sunrises, the dolphins, even the gales and lightning and thunderstorms are things you will miss. What more can you ask of life than the light, tight circle of family and thought and horizon?' But the voice beneath the noise wasn't very loud.

We were now approaching Plymouth Heads. Another launch purred up. It contained the snowy-haired Commodore of the Royal Western Yacht Club.

'Hurry, hurry,' he urged. 'The press are waiting. You're late already.'

Our boss the weather shook his head as for the first

time for two and a half years we hurried for a man-made appointment.

A Bobcat with gleaming white hulls and sails reached cheerily up to greet her Oceanic relation *Anneliese*. The wake from four stubby, sturdy hulls frothed and mingled. Both boats were Bill O'Brien designs, works of art more useful than poetry. Sailing boats now filled the water all around us. We peered through sail gaps and saw land close by. We were almost there.

I wished we could stay in the decompression chamber of the outer harbour awhile, but there was no time.

Colin said, 'Let's put up the spinnaker and sail into the harbour in style!' But Jimmy had spilt his chocolate drink on the white part last week and anyway too many things were happening all at once.

Our six-knot life was speeding up towards an emotional sound barrier. A crowd of faces was coming into focus. Colin looked for our friends and wasn't sure if he'd recognize them after all this time. The holes in my crochet dress from Tahiti seemed rather large. Our private world was being invaded.

The stout ropes on the end of Eve and Jimmy's safety harnesses dealt with the excitement as capably as they had dealt with the storms, as the children strained at the end of them and jumped up and down in the cockpit.

Three weeks of sea mist and fog had stolen our equatorial suntans, and it was the onlookers in sunny Plymouth who looked as though they had just come back from a round the world voyage. The bright red mooring buoy to which we were shown reflected pink against *Anneliese*'s hulls, surprising stowaway sea creatures who had never seen such a strange thing before. Friendly people were all around us. Hands helped the children off *Anneliese* into a launch to go ashore.

Colin looked worried. '*How do we know the mooring chain under the buoy isn't rusted through?*'

'Oh well, there must be a time when you can stop worrying!'

This was it. The voyage had ended. For the first time

in our whole sea journey we were leaving the boat unattended and on an apparent lee shore. The spring of the six-hour watch was broken. *Anneliese* couldn't come any further with us. For the first time for two and a half years we were leaving our friend and partner behind.

Jimmy's pink Peanuts blanket of security nearly fell in the sea as he goggled up at all the people. Then all at once we began to recognize some of the faces around us, just as at sea we would stand at dusk and recognize a few of our friendly navigational stars from a skyful.

We walked shakily up the steps shadowed by the cameras leaning over us from the jetty above. The BBC were there and ITN and all the newspapers. They got some lovely smiles as we recognized our friends. Bionic eighty-year-old Cousin Katherine, the very first person who had dared to come out with us when we had first started sailing – when she had survived sailing backwards out through the Needles channel in an embarrassed *Anneliese* – now rushed up and gave us all a hug and slipped a sachet of luxury herbal shampoo down the front of my dress.

We looked back at our friend *Anneliese*. She seemed to be enjoying herself bobbing gently on her shiny red mooring. Sailing up the English Channel, the only sign she had shown of all she had been through were the few scribbles on the walls the children had done. Now we noticed that the Australian antifouling on her hulls had been delicately replaced by weed, and thousands of illegal barnacle immigrants had stowed their way home to Britain. Also those self-steering bolts, pride of Colin and a Barbados sugar factory, now wept rusty tears even through the fine new white paint we'd just brushed on the vanes.

'*Anneliese* was so nice and comfortable, and in port it is so lovely on board her,' Colin said wistfully as we were driven away.

At last we had finished being loaded into cameras and the newsmen who had been very kind to us all the way around the world had gone away. It had all been rather alarming. We'd been presented with a proof copy of my first book with all the nude pictures in it and we'd thought: OHHHHHHH! Whatever will Auntie Fe say?

At a giant press conference they had grilled us for two hours, reviving us frequently with champagne. They had asked, among a crowd of other questions, what we thought about all the terrible news, the crises ashore – the petrol shortages, the strikes. Perhaps they had forgotten that there are always shortages at sea anyway.

'NUDE SAILOR REVEALS ALL!' captioned *The Sun* next day.

The beautiful seals had been lost. Priceless pictures of iguanas taken in the Galapagos Islands still gathered dust under the sleeping desk of some South American airport official. Glorious sunsets attracted as much editorial attention as a Technicolor advertisement for jam. Exotic islands were tossed into grey wastepaper baskets.

But pictures of bare human skin, the commonest thing of all, had survived both the ordeal of the airfreight offices and the interest of the editors. We'd woken up that morning to find our sunburnt bodies curling around many paragraphs. My bare legs were startling the tired faces of politicians on the opposite page. Headlines were made of the most normal thing of all and little more notice was taken of our real adventure than of the discovery of the round world several hundred years ago.

But the long legs lived only in the newspapers. The curtains of sweeping skirts had finally drawn around the mini and people were walking as well as waiting on platforms.

Many things had changed, but not people's kindness.

'What is it?' Jimmy asked later that day.

'It's STEAK!' Eve explained. 'And real CHIPS!'

The manager of Plymouth's Berni Inn beamed solicitously. The meal was a present to us from him. But now our taste buds, trained by weeks of dried soup, could manage only one chip at a time, savouring each one like a meal in itself.

'Didn't you like it?' The manager bent anxiously over.

'Oh yes! Thank you.' But it was a bit like eating a mirage. Our mouths were not full of steak and chips, but fantasies.

Afterwards Jimmy, the clip of his sea-going safety harness still clanking faithfully behind him, followed me cautiously into Mothercare. An assistant in a blue checked overall approached.

'What age is he?' she asked, then came back with several pairs of shoes. By luck, one pair seemed to think it fitted. But Jimmy didn't agree at all.

'No, no, no!' he shouted. He looked at his feet as though an accident had happened to them. Howls never heard by the fish in the wildest ocean were now heard by the assistants in Mothercare. Pregnant ladies peeped nervously out through the woollies.

That night he celebrated by peeing on the thick green carpet of a room in the Holiday Inn. He thought it was grass. The doors of Plymouth's biggest supermarket slid open by themselves. A column of baked beans flashed like a red port buoy as we passed. There were rows and rows of cabbages and crisps and people.

'Are those ladies for sale too?' Eve asked.

We passed a hundred *Anneliese*fuls of biscuits and beaming apricots such as we had eaten during the long dark watches at the beginning of our voyage. We used to kid ourselves that we were lightening the boat's burden with our midnight munching, each burp a help.

The lady reporter's eyes and ballpoint rolled to follow us around the shining supermarket. Everything was in pence as if in a world of rich children's pocket money. Bright lights shone on the edible stars of the departments. Soft music played to the mood of rows of tinned meats, the chorus of this strange musical show.

'Have the prices changed much?' the lady reporter asked, scribbling away for her woman's page. I couldn't say much. But she looked as if she had already decided what I should say anyway.

A week after coming ashore the sea still seemed an

easier place to live than on land. We had to go to a launderette for the first time, find money and powders and bleaches. But at sea I'd never had to do any real washing. I had just tied a rolling hitch around the nappies and dirty clothes and thrown them over the side, towed them for several miles and then had hung them up in the rigging to dry. Now our socks missed the fish.

The sea seemed safer too. Driving up to London in a friend's car was more frightening than a force 10 gale in kindly *Anneliese*.

'Oh this wretched 50 mph speed limit!' moaned our friend as we sped along. But for us who were used to going at 6 knots, it was terrifyingly fast.

Most of all, the sea had never been as alarming as the prospect of the first lecture we had to give ...

'We decided you would like to get it over *before* dinner after all,' said the chairman, adjusting the microphones among the gleaming sideplates. The huge sports stadium with its boxing ring in the centre and the tables all round grew more enormous. I wished I could swap places with the boxers.

I looked over at Colin. His cufflinks were glinting and his hands shook a little as we stood up. I knew that he too had been relying on practising silently through the consommé and pork and apple. Now eight hundred polite pairs of eyes above eight hundred spotless dinner jackets looked enquiringly our way. They hadn't even had a drink to help them swallow our first-ever speech – luckily they were nearly as cheerful as the dolphins who'd been our friends at sea. An hour later it was all over and questions were mixing with food and drink and fun.

'Mummy, Mummy – why aren't you licking your plate like you do at sea?' I thought I heard a little voice enquire. The gravy gazed remorselessly up from the plates. I thought of eight hundred elegant tongues licking at the delicate patterns.

'What will happen in the months ahead?' I wondered. 'Will we ever become civilized enough to manage on land?'

THREE

The ballet of the mice

'THERE'S NOBODY ON WATCH!'

Colin was fast asleep beside me. I started violently in the sleeping bag and fumbled for the end of my safety harness. Instead my hand grasped the lead of an ancient electric fire.

'Anyone turning the doorknob rearranges the furniture,' Colin had proclaimed proudly on discovering No. 14 Lexham Gardens.

The landlord too was small. He was round and light brown with a moustache and a mouth both of which smiled all day, and the Queen's head imprinted on the palms of his hands. His building was just his wallet. It was neatly divided into small compartments out of which he could extract his cash each week.

'Were you lonely, not knowing anyone in England after being thrown out of Uganda by General Amin?' we asked, after hearing his story.

'Oh *no*,' he smiled. 'Not so bad. Luckily my son has been sub-postmaster in Isleworth for fifteen years, and my brother is owning the hotel next door!'

He scrutinized our first rent cheque, earned from our lecture, and began to look embarrassed. 'Please,' he whispered digging in his pocket and proffering a piece of paper, 'please sign this form. I couldn't have it said that I'm cramming whoole Breetish family with children into one room.'

It was much smaller than our 30-foot *Anneliese*. But since we had to be in London for book promotion, we needed something like a little 'landboat' to feel at home. But it wasn't just a 'whoole Breetish family' who lived in our room. The person on the outside of the narrow lower bunk bed on which Colin and I both slept had permanent bruises from falling out each night!

This entertainment was watched by hundreds of bright little eyes.

'SQUEAK ... SQUEAK! Perhaps they've come in out of the cold,' our room mates said as they peeped out at us. Yes, the mice were kind-hearted and tolerant to the new creatures who had invaded their home. We even began to be useful to them in some ways.

I woke up one morning to find our small wooden Tongan canoe, which we had hung up to remind us of the Pacific, lurching about on the wall, seemingly by magic. Then the magic became visible as four little feet running frantically from end to end, delicate fan ears quivering, tiny pink toes clinging on to the edges of the canoe. He allowed us to rescue him. But how he got up there in the first place remained his secret.

During the voyage the children had unpacked two hundred and ninety-three Kelloggs Varipacks one day and made themselves a cereal sandpit. Now the mice seemed to have just as much fun with one packet of cornflakes. Fun was a vitamin on which they thrived. Sugar bags rustled into action, still life into movement. One day Colin bought a fluorescent flickering light paperweight to give to a friend. It sat on the table all night and they thought it was a Fairy Tinkerbell for mice. The room became the sound effects for a million-dollar nature film. In the end, after many months with this as a little land base, we thought it polite to leave.

By now the rule of the sea had shaken hands with the rule of the land. There were no vertical walls of water in London; no brilliant patches of green where a wild sea had whipped itself into a frenzy; no storms, no low leaden lid of a Southern Ocean sky. There were no icebergs over the horizon. But instead the children discovered that there was a bite behind the tempting glow of orange bars of the electric fire; that steep stairs followed each other up like sheep but were more dangerous; that flickering boxes could explode if you poked fingers inside to find the cowboys. And we learnt how to be careful in friendly Yacht Clubs where the Commodores didn't realize that now one small sherry could make us lurch around as much as a large wave.

Each day was an adventure.

'I've arranged a television programme for you,' our agent said one day. 'You must earn your living you know.'

'Hello little girl – will you be my friend?' Eve asked conspiratorially. 'Please play with me.'

'My god! She doesn't realize it's a monitor,' one of the Thames Television studio technicians gasped, as Eve went on happily talking to herself. David Nixon, sitting beside her, smiled and made it all seem part of his magic.

'Whose Baby?' was a television programme where a panel had to guess which children belonged to which parents. Colin and I were placed discreetly behind screens. A make-up girl bent bosom and brush towards Colin's nose. Eve and Jimmy thought it great fun. By the end of the programme Arthur Askey, Jimmy Young and Charlie Chester were all sitting on the floor helping our children construct a castle from the giant Lego set the studio had given them.

Our agent was saving up for a new house so we did a lot of television and radio work during the next few months. It was strange to appear in so many thousand 'sitting rooms', yet never sit on the sofa or meet the people. But the children loved it. They gargled during the Eamonn Andrews Show and he might as well have been speaking from County Limerick. Pete Murray turned pale and gazed nervously as Jimmy rummaged around the plugs and the multi-thousand-pound equipment at 'Open House', threatening to put the whole of Broadcasting House into silence.

'Don't let them touch the microphones,' the floor manager would invariably hiss about fifty seconds before the start of a telly programme.

'What are those?' Eve and Jimmy would wonder under the boring adult torrent of words of the interview.

'Oh YES . . . How lovely!' – and the floor manager's idea would be put enthusiastically into action.

Tough soundmen and cameramen who had probably braved shellfire on location grew rigid and hollow-eyed as they gazed at us in the studio. One of the biggest ever mail bags was received by BBC South on the occasion that the programme had ended with Eve and Jimmy both clutching the same glass of water over the lap of an even more glassy-eyed interviewer. 'Which one won the tug o' war?' they asked.

Back in Southampton an onlooker gazed at our boat amazed. 'How did she float at all?' he asked.

Anneliese was out of the water at last. We had sailed her back to Southampton and now she was in Willment's shipyard, outside her birthplace, Bill O'Brien's shed. The mud where we had first met him, where it had all begun, still remained. A new generation of swans carried on the tradition of slaloming among the bitter black warps of the jetties.

Sleeping bags weak from their efforts to keep out Antarctic cold, books written in fungus and English, clothes with mould embroidery, plus a thousand treasures of sea-weary junk, now a challenge for Miss Imagination competitions, all came off the boat.

Anneliese stood quite still on stumpy hulls. She looked as sound as the day she had first let us climb on board. But we had promised her that if she brought us back safely from Cape Horn, she should have the finest treatment. So we now left her with Bill O'Brien looking forward to having her teak decks, on whom so many flying fish had landed, replaced with shining new strips of wood. She had been invited to appear at the next Earls Court Boat Show and wanted to look her best.

The voyage had stopped, but time hadn't. My first birthday ashore for years would be the birthday also of my first book. As I creaked up the stairs to the publishers I felt so proud that it was being published. But also scared because unknown strangers I could never see, or touch or know one single thing about, would know me. We were being brought out of the undergrowth of life. Even the stern-faced librarians I had always got into trouble with through not returning their charges, would have copies.

On the publisher's windowsill my own face, with one or two fly-droppings on it, welcomed me with an inappropriate expression. The cover picture looked bright and cheerful, keeping the secret of all the arguments and discussions surrounding its choice. *Rosie Darling* was really a member of the family as well as a book. It had been born at sea just as my son Jimmy had, and we had sent it home as our representative when we still had 19,000 miles of the wildest seas in the world to sail through. I'd always been determined it would be a survivor. Even if the manuscript lived thereafter only in the lavender-scented drawer of an indulgent friend. Now it was being published! A month later came the first booksigning session.

'What a *dreadful* shop!' a loud female voice behind me boomed. 'Where do you sell the biros, dear?'

'I'm – I'm not sure ... sorry ...' I stammered, realizing she was talking to me.

The lady in the large pink hat gave me a sub-zero glance before disappearing back again into the Saturday morning rush. 'Another ignorant sales girl. Where *do* they get them from?' I heard her mutter as she went.

The manager of W. H. Smith's, in a chameleon suit the colour of many shelves, averted his eyes to hide his smile with the biros. The publisher's representatives bent over my desk and tried to look like customers buying *Rosie Darling*. There were rows and rows of my book everywhere. It was a mad multiplication of pictures and words and ideas.

'How can they think they're lucky to get a copy if there are so many strewn about?' Colin observed. '... Love to Gladys ... To Mildred and Tom ... Happy Sailing! ... Best wishes ... Happy Birthday Stephen ...'

'Fifty-five copies gone already!' whispered the manager gleefully. But still the area around the signing session seemed the emptiest in the shop. People passed by looking at their watches, at their children, at their shoes. The pride of publishing a book seemed less now. W. H. Smith's was like Battersea Dogs' Home. Full of books hoping to be chosen. And they weren't even free to good homes!

We were sadly missing *Anneliese* who was still in the boatyard being titivated. But for the time being the book was our transport. We went to the Frankfurt Book Fair and met a paper forest of publishers. There were as many publishers as I had once thought there were books in the whole world. We went to Scotland and ate our first haggis. We went to Paris as the guests of *Paris Match*.

'You'll recognize our reporter because she'll be carrying a copy of our magazine,' they'd told us, not saying very much for their circulation. The charming blonde who met us introduced herself – and promptly flung her copy of *Paris Match* into the wastepaper basket. Our nights were spent in pink blancmange hotel beds, our days being herded gently by the magazine's sheepdog camera lenses.

The champagne had just settled in our veins when it was time to fly home again. The security man at the airport looked suspiciously at my large bulging handbag.

'*Montrez moi*,' he said with bomb-exposing cool, and unzipped the bag.

'MON DIEU!'

All his training deserted him. He grew rigid with shock. Then he carefully put in his hand and withdrew, not a gun – but a pink potty. It was just Jimmy's special loo, which always travelled with him!

FOUR

Ghost of a crooked house

The gales had passed. Cape Horn sat safely in Colin's photographs. At sea the strain had always begun to show after the storm was over. Three days after Cape Horn we'd had the most terrific row about how to hang Jimmy's vest up on the rigging. Now it was the same. We'd been working hard and made much of. Our agent's house was almost paid for. But what purpose lay ahead for us? Which way were we going? Once in London, to the mice's surprise I threw a whole cup of coffee over the cover of my second book pinned on the wall. And one day Colin pounded my Timex watch to pulp with a hammer!

I didn't think Colin got enough credit for his pictures, for filming rare birds that had never been to Lucie Clayton's, and I thought it sad that only the Autumn Reader's Digest Bestseller Non-fiction Collection used his photographs in colour. I wondered what the sea, the sky, the seals, the exotic islands would think, if they knew they were being represented to the world as black and white and grey, instead of blue and green, red and the thousand other colours that even a colour film has to struggle to capture.

The next journey Jimmy's pink potty made was the following week when we all went up to Lancashire to do a lecture for the Round Table. *Anneliese* sailed a last time across the white screen they had rigged up. Then the lights came on

'Ladies and gentlemen,' I began. 'If when we were eating our rusty baked beans and chips cooked in the baby's cod liver oil, sailing up the South Atlantic, we had known that we would be lucky enough to be here with you tonight, we wouldn't have been so ...'

Suddenly something white shot out of my mouth. It whistled close by the ear of the gentleman in the front row. He swatted at his head as if a fly had been bothering him. My tongue found a black glowering hole in my bottom jaw before the next sentence ... My God – my Evo Stik crown tooth had come out at last. But luckily no one seemed to notice. Somebody put a red carnation down my bosom and everyone cheered, captivated as much by many delicious pints of beer as by us.

The next item on the bill was the striptease and a large girl came up covered by spotlights instead of clothes, with her tits pointing nor' nor' east and nor' nor' west. Two voices behind us were raised slightly above the music.

'What's a Yorkshire man like you doing in Lancashire?' one asked.

'Oh,' came the answer immediately, 'missionary work – just missionary work!'

At three a.m. a great black Rolls-Royce came and scooped up the merry local Mayor and us to take us back to our beds for the night.

All this was a great change from the peace of the sea. We were glad we had brought our little tent with us. Next day our Round Table friends took us off in their car and reluctantly left us in a gleaming trough of mud in a lane at the bottom of Pendle Hill. We puffed force 9 as we gave piggy-backs to the rucksacks, two saucepans, the tent and the children. The mountain sheep we passed looked most astonished.

During the night the tent shook to the shriek of wind and many other things. I remembered the famous witches of Pendle Hill and that it was Hallowe'en. I was sure they were kindly and wouldn't mind us sleeping on their beautiful hill. That night I was surrounded by wise friends I'd never known I had. They were singing to me and calling me, calling me towards some future. Our tent was being guarded by unseen sheep and broomsticks. I felt I would never be alone again.

During the night I was shown the fierce gleam of an

idea which I'd have to follow. Be careful, it may not be what you think, the friendly voices warned. I looked again. But it was gone and all that was left in my mind was a poem:

Gracious Goddess
Hear me! I entreat thee,
For I feel the dark swift arrows
Of some unknown unenlightened enemy,
Thou who knowst the hearts of men,
Shield me I implore thee
Thou who see'st all. Thou who knowst all,
Break the arrows in their flight,
Return them unto their Sender
Gracious Goddess
BLESS ME BLESS ME BLESS ME ...

By morning I still felt restless. But the idea was gone along with the dancing footmarks of the friendly witches. I had been given some work to do, I had been given some strength: what work, what strength I wasn't sure. But I felt sure those wise, wise voices of the night would help.

Next day we travelled down south again and began to discover that there can be as many gales and depressions in the business world as there are at sea. And that wind isn't the only thing that changes.

'*Anneliese* can't go in the Earls Court show after all,' the officials told us. 'She's not a commercial yacht.'

Anneliese herself didn't take much more notice of this than she had of the 60-foot waves near Cape Horn. Our agent too didn't seem to mind. The books would still be sold at the show. There'd still be plenty of free booze.

To cheer ourselves up we decided to go to Ireland for Christmas to see the ghosts of my goats and the old black mare I'd had as a child. I hoped they wouldn't mind that it was my knickers on the front of *Reveille* that were paying for this trip.

We brought our bicycles with us to Ireland. Authors

only get paid twice a year, so your paypacket seems large, if you don't think too far ahead. Anyway we'd snatched the first royalties from the pages of *Rosie Darling* and had gone and bought the finest transport we'd ever had ashore.

I'd always longed for an open-roof car. Now at last I had my open-air set of wheels. But they were two. Eve and Jimmy sat on little red seats on the crossbars and had time to count grey squirrels and have long discussions with us. The world had slowed down to the six-knot speed of enchantment again.

The children made a new friend at the start of our journey to Ireland. A giant cat lives in the ladies' lavatory at Paddington Station looked after by three devoted attendants. People are only tolerated in this loo. Pictures of Tiddles adorn the lavatory walls instead of graffiti. Larger and larger portraits and larger and larger baskets hold her frame each year. She arrived at Paddington among the suitcases and hurrying feet, tens of thousands of tins of Whiskas ago. Now, we were told, she only comes out for a walk on platform one at six o'clock in the morning. Anyway she only opened one yellow eye when Jimmy with his long blond hair was smuggled in by Eve to meet her. Mobile Ireland, buffet car and all, starts on the cat's platform one, not far from my old London bedsitter many years and a thousand dreams away.

An old woman who reminded me of my grandmother, who had brought me up, was sitting next to the window reading a large-print book not half so full of stories as herself. From time to time she'd raise her head and gaze intently out of the window. The countryside was changing every moment, yet always the same in the black blackness of the December evening. The darkness seemed stolen from the summer nights.

Next morning Eve and Jimmy, with mouths full of breakfast toast and eyes full of Ireland, came out on deck in time to see the ship sailing up the River Lee with dolls' houses on either side. We steamed slowly past Cobb along the trail of *Anneliese*'s first ever voyage – to Ireland. At Cork docks were signposts which must cheer up the printers immensely because they all have to be written in English which people understand and Irish, which is their language.

We passed the Cork School of Music where I had learnt to play the Irish harp, though not how to avoid banging it on the knees of old ladies when I carried it in its case on the bus. But the sweetshop on the way there had been demolished. Only the ghosts of the sugary buns I had bought there remained.

Grian-an in Co. Limerick was the house my grandmother had built and lived in. The windows were crooked but sunny. The water was soft, but what went out from the sink came up the bath plug hole. It was still much the same outside as I remembered, though shrunken with my age.

Inside, the old house was both brighter and shabbier, more hopeless and happier. The wooden floor which Biddy had polished with her heart and knees was covered with coloured rugs now. A tone deaf piano stood against a cracked wall where a bright poster hung. The 'red' kitchen still had the black ceiling bequeathed by its range. The 'blue' kitchen still had luxury mouseholes in the corners. But now a pyramid of eighteen cats slept in a cardboard box beside the door and dogs' legs mixed with the chair legs standing under the table. The old tennis court had become a haycourt so coarse in winter that the cows in the surrounding field didn't even bother to get through the broken-down fence.

We had a lovely Christmas and were spoilt by my stepmother Marianne, who knew that Eve and Jimmy and Colin and I appreciated it even more than other people who came to see her. We all got drunk, including my half-brother Gerald whose long legs we had to chase round and round the garden to catch before he collapsed. And we had a splendid Christmas party in the drawing room. Lots of people, the same yet not the same as I remembered, came and wine was spilt on an old carpet which still bore the marks of my grandmother's wheelchair.

On Boxing Day we cycled over to visit a roaring fire

and some friends in Shanagolden. Years ago I used to drive the little donkey Jeanette along the same road in her trap to do the weekly shopping. When we got to the shop I used to unhitch her and she'd lie down and roll in the middle of the road scratching her back on the pebbly surface, while any traffic just pulled up. Or she'd nibble the long field of the verges.

A week later our little holiday was over. We travelled back to Cork on the train with the bicycles leaning against crates of new-born chicks in the guard's van. In the carriage a Holy Sister with a cheerful expression was reading Alistair Maclean inside her Book of Prayer.

At Cork Station Jimmy rushed into the Ladies by mistake and disturbed a nun sitting on the loo. He thought it was his friend from the train and grinned. She smiled an angelic smile back. I yanked him out, embarrassed, muttering apologies. It had almost been better when we used to carry his pink potty in my handbag.

There wasn't time to steam back to England, so we thought we'd try out Ireland's newest airport.

'How far is Cork Airport?' we asked a cheery old Corkman.

'Sure 'tis only a mile.'

We cycled on for an hour. Another old man was clipping the verges.

'Can you tell me how far it is to Cork Airport please?'

He beamed reassuringly: 'Oh, it's only a mile, only a mile.'

A short-horn cow peered pityingly at us through a gap in the hedge. We cycled on. Then came another hill almost as high as the clouds. If the Airport was along here, the planes wouldn't have much taking off to do.

Eve and Jim sat in front on the bikes, with pampered unpedalling feet. The bike chains groaned. The rucksacks clung on grimly behind. The road looked too new and smooth to be so difficult to cycle along. The gradient was disguised in best quality tarmac. All at once we saw a man who looked a bit like an airport official. What a relief!

'How far is it to the Airport please?' Colin asked, his sweaty face brightening.

'Oh sure 'tis only a mile.'

An Irish mile perhaps! ...

The pipe of the man in the booking office was almost put out by our gasping question: *'Has ... has the flight gone?'*

'Sure it won't be going for another six hours,' he said getting out his matches. 'Make yerselves at home.'

Half an hour later I started getting presents. Jimmy kept arriving with more and more bars of chocolate, Rollos, mints and crisps. Marianne had certainly packed a generous box of treats.

'For you and Daddy,' he beamed with super bright cheeks.

Colin, ex-chocolate champion, famous for eating 293 bars of chocolate while crossing the Atlantic, began to recover from his exhaustion.

Then suddenly a large lady with permed layers of ginger hair and enormous black buttons on her cardigan arrived. She looked extremely angry!

FIVE

False gods

We had always had to pay half fare for our bicycles on the trains, but on Aer Lingus, Ireland's friendly airline, they travelled free. All we had to do was to take the pedals off and turn them inwards. It was just as well that we remembered to change them round again before we cycled from Heathrow to London. It was a long way at three a.m. Jimmy fell asleep on his seat on the way and Colin had to cycle behind my bike and pick up his little red wellington boots when they fell off.

Two days later, the bicycles had recovered enough to take us to the opening of Earls Court Boat Show. What a sight! Boats for every ocean, boats for every dream. All but *Anneliese* gleamed at the show. There was also a feast, a banquet of boating equipment. There were cleats with chrome icing, spotless Technicolor warps, and not a single barnacle among a hundred hulls.

On the second day of the show, I saw the *Daily Express* page one picture of us arriving at Earls Court on our bicycles with the children on the floor in the ladies' lavatory with a large footprint on it.

'I wish there was a special day for exhibitors to see the show properly,' Colin mourned, shackled to our stand.

This stand was in a passage in the desolate wastes of the Show. A lady stood in the centre of the passage selling programmes as people came in. Passers-by were usually either in a hurry to see the boats in the show, or in a hurry to get home for tea. With a bit of luck Eve or Jimmy would trip some of them up and they'd come to see us as we stood behind huge piles of *Children of Cape Horn* – the book of the ocean written thousands of miles out at sea, as much a part of the waves as any of the gleaming hulls around us.

Friends at whose Lyme Regis home Colin and I had spent our honeymoon came specially to the Show to see us. They were lovely people. But their visit collided with an invitation to a party in the hall's plush apartments upstairs. 'There are some important businessmen you must meet,' said a gravelly PR man at our elbows.

Something in our souls must have given way. Instead of asking our old friends out to dinner, we said goodbye hastily to them and followed the trail of the false gods upstairs.

The red-faced man I was talking to a little later looked a bit drunk. His hand steadied itself on my waist. He might be a reporter, I thought.

'My name's Hyams,' he confided.

'What do you do, Mr Hyams?' I asked politely.

'Oh, I'm in building.' He looked glazedly in search of the glass in his other hand and went to fill it up.

'That's *Harry Hyams,* the multimillionaire, the one who built *Centre Point,*' the PR man whispered loudly from behind, adding that nearly everyone else at this party was a millionaire too.

But what did we need a millionaire for? Anyway they looked quite ordinary to us. They all just seemed to be trying to enjoy themselves in sober suits and unsober faces. Their richness, I thought, must be hidden in their souls or in their wallets.

But also there, looking like a star as bright as those she used to navigate her way through the sky by, was Sheila Scott. She said she'd had to part with her beloved aeroplane because flying around the world was too expensive. 'You're lucky,' she said wistfully. 'At least your fuel is free.'

'There's a *very* nice picture of you in the paper today!' The man's leery eyes said more than his words as he shoved page three of the tabloid in front of me. There I was again; walking down the decks of *Anneliese* carrying baby Jimmy who, with a nappy on, was wearing more clothes than myself.

'It must be the twentieth time they've printed this picture,' Colin muttered.

'It's beautiful,' eulogized an editor over his shoulder. 'It must have been taken with sea-scoured lenses.' I just thought I looked rather fat.

Suddenly vibrations in the loud room changed. A man who looked as though he lived many lives at once came up and spoke to the PR man. He had an authority that you couldn't buy with a frilly dinner shirt and that the scraggy jacket with the half-done-up buttons couldn't disguise. He looked at us keenly with wide-spaced brown eyes, one eyebrow higher than the other. There was an almost devilish twinkle about that strange face as he invited us up to Norfolk to visit him. Half an hour later a handful of golden carrots had hidden the sea horizon from our eyes.

'Have a free newspaper, love,' said the guard, handing me a *Sun* from the pile he was loading into the guard's van.

Three hours later we were in a green flat land, more strange to us than the Galapagos. It was Norfolk.

Our new guardian only believed in working on 'Wednesday afternoons!' But by the time we had known him for two weeks we already had a solicitor, an accountant, a company, a car, a cottage, a business manager – all in two Wednesday afternoons! Could we ever survive in a world spinning around as fast as this, I wondered?

There we were, settled in a cottage in the wilds of Norfolk instead of in the wilds of the ocean. We had a sea of green instead of a sea of blue around us now. We had clothes lines instead of mooring warps and there were weeds in the garden instead of under the hulls. The only thing the same was that in this cottage, as at sea, there still was no bathroom.

A local farmer's plough churned the enormous vegetable area into straight brown lines in deference to our ignorance as gardeners. And so, until the weeds came up again and gave us away, we were able to pretend we had planted the garden with great care. The only thing we ever really grew successfully was one magnificent lettuce. Then workmen painting the window frames of the cottage dropped spots of black paint on it.

Eve thought that going to school was a bigger adventure than going to sea. But she soothed the harassed teachers down as she had us at sea. She would say something like: 'What a pretty brooch you're wearing.' And then smile until the classroom frost melted.

Anyway, the headmaster was in love with the new golden Pontiac I used to drive Eve to school in. It was a car which seemed to breathe in round the corners of the narrow Norfolk roads. I found driving very frightening now. For the ocean is a very broad road compared even to the M1.

Things were still very strange on land. Neat little beds now decorated the children's room. But every night the mattresses had to be put on the floor for them to sleep. And Colin and I gave a good home to an ancient double bed with a private life of its own. But it was all just for show. We really slept better on the floor.

Outside the countryside looked green and peaceful. But for some reason the peace stayed with the grass and I felt restless and uneasy. The countryside was flat, oh so flat. But I saw mountains. I saw the sky-stroking shape of Pendle Hill and its voices. The voices seemed now to be saying: 'Go back. Go back to *Anneliese*. Money isn't eternal. Money isn't everything. Go back to *Anneliese*. It's your last chance. Your life is a walk away from innocence. Soon it'll be too far, too late to turn back.'

But I really didn't listen. I was dazzled by the glitter of the beautiful Pontiac our new benefactor had given me.

SIX

Blue films and Carnation milk – never!

One evening a neighbour appeared at the door of our cottage. 'Don't worry if you feels sick tonight,' he said, his round red face smiling benignly. 'It's just the poison ... I'll be spraying it on the field behind your cottage.'

We thanked him shakily for warning us and went to the window to shut out the healthy country air.

My uneasiness kept growing like an evergreen tree. Most of our patron's winters were occupied taking cabinet ministers or oil tycoons or film producers out shooting, usually not at each other, which was just as well since he said he was negotiating the film rights of my books with them. One day he asked us to come along with the shoot. Some of the American oil men seemed fierce as they carried what looked like sub machine guns. But they only hurt our minds.

The fat ducks swam slowly, expectantly, across the pond for their daily feed of biscuit. Keepers shooed them up into the air. They rose heavily, reluctantly. A few minutes later the birds were all dead. It had been difficult to miss. There had to be a prize for hitting the sky instead of the ducks.

But there was scarcely time for my uneasiness to settle where I could see it. Colin and I spent most of his birthday in a beauty salon in London, being crimped and titivated for glossy photographs for a new teenage magazine. The soft warm air that dried his hair in the salon was very different from the wild wind that had howled through the dark curls on his last birthday, 300 miles off Cape Horn.

We went off to Holland to promote the books in Dutch and visited Amsterdam where they seemed to sell sex aids like sticks of rock and the people understood our English better than our Dutch.

Then before our weeds could grow again we were off on a paperback tour of Britain. Being in paperback seemed like a Pulitzer Prize to me. And now that they weren't so expensive the books themselves would lead more adventurous lives. They could lurk among the gingernuts in the supermarkets. They could be pawed and whirled on swirling stands on railway platforms. They would even be sold at Boots, so that if reading them gave you a headache, the remedy would be close at hand.

Local television stations around England seemed to be like little separate kingdoms, ruled and peopled by their own producers, presenters, personalities. Southern, lazing by the River Itchen in Southampton, seemed jolly and sexy, Tyne Tees particularly village-like, Yorkshire ambitious, HTV intellectual. The BBC stations, manufacturer of Britain's biggest export, the English voice, were all more serious.

'Party?' said the paperback publishers of *Children of Cape Horn* a few weeks later. 'What party? If we gave a party for every book of ours that did well, we should make no money.'

'BOLLOCKS!' exclaimed Colin startlingly – and then his only concern became which day to have it.

'Thursday,' said our Norfolk magician.

'Wednesday,' said Colin, and promptly arranged a party at the Savoy.

Two weeks later Savoyees with manners even more splendid than their uniforms welcomed 150 people minus one into the grand Gondolier Room with its diamond chandeliers. Half way through the evening one of them rushed up saying there was a telephone call for us.

It was Harold Wilson: 'Eh, I'm sorry I can't come my dear. But I've been held up by t'Queen at t'Palace.' But he popped in later almost unnoticed.

Anyway we had a lovely dinner and the effect of the huge magnums of champagne didn't matter. The carpets were so soft that if you fell over, it didn't hurt. But I really felt I was orbiting in outer space in an atmosphere not our own.

Leaning across Colin I tried to hear what was coming through the receiver. He was inviting a 'very important person' to dinner. My ears scorched as I listened to the voices.

'Next Tuesday,' said Christopher Lee at the other end. He had such a lovely voice. I thought it was a shame to have cast him as Dracula. Anyway Colin rushed off to book a table for lunch at the Dorchester.

Next Tuesday we turned up at our joint lawyer's offices to meet Christopher Lee at twelve o'clock as arranged. But the lawyer wasn't wearing his usual cheerful expression when we arrived. He seemed to be on the brink of second childishness and about to suck his thumb with nerves.

'Mr Lee was here waiting for you *last* Tuesday,' he gasped at last. 'He waited quite a while.'

Poor Christopher Lee, I thought. I was sure he hadn't often been kept waiting a week for lunch!

'But what didn't you like about this film?' the presenter of 'Kaleidoscope' insisted as she leaned over us in her BBC studio. We were bad people to ask really. We had been suffering from cinematic malnutrition for so long while at sea, that we now enjoyed almost all films. Anyway Gregory Peck was going to take us out to dinner that evening and it seemed rude not to be polite about your host.

The film we were now reviewing for the BBC was *The Dove* directed by Gregory Peck. It is about a young man who sailed around the world in a boat of this name, alone except for a temperamental ginger tomcat. At an island on the way he meets a girl and her love nearly stops the voyage as much as the danger does. He is nearly drowned, the cat is. At one stage he actually set fire to his boat so that he wouldn't have to go on. But he does! We'd had to go to the cinema at nine o'clock in the morning and had sat among rows of journalists with twitching pencils. We'd felt very decadent coming out of the cinema again in broad daylight.

In the evening Percival Pontiac chauffeured by Colin's hairdresser took us to the Royal Première. 'Wear your wet-look catsuit,' our business manager had insisted, thinking that all this fuss might make the ink run easier on future film contracts. The catsuit had been designed for me by a black belt karate expert dressmaker, who specialized in show biz clothes. The first time we had gone to his den we'd seen various garments hanging on a rail near the window. The legs and sleeves had all seemed far too long.

'He can't be much good!' Colin had muttered. It turned out the clothes were for Procol Harum, all of whom are about seven feet tall!

The real life mother of the actor, Joseph Bottom, playing the young sailor was playing the role of his Mum in the film. And at the end of the performance when his voyage had ended and he was coming back to his family, the audience heard a loud sob coming from the Royal Circle. It was Joseph. He was a long way from his home in California after all! Mark Phillips who was sitting beside him leaned over and patted him on the back. Perhaps he thought it wasn't quite 'stiff upper lip'!

During dinner at the Savoy afterwards Gregory Peck looked worried. 'To sail around the world you need one Dove,' he explained. 'To film someone sailing around the world, you need eight Doves and it all costs ten times as much. Films are as risky as sailing. To start with, *The Dove* must pay for this dinner!' We were still eating iced melon and cream at three a.m.

The morning was still the end of yesterday. But by afternoon we had bathed the black circles under our eyes and were creeping off to Buckingham Palace. The nude statues in the corridors of the Palace were not at all what we had expected, but the staff were all dressed formally to compensate.

We'd been asked to give out some of the Duke of Edinburgh's Gold Awards for him. Shaking roomsful of white gloves which hid hands that had been canoeing, mountaineering, exploring, looking after people in need, was an awe-inspiring experience.

Afterwards I told Prince Philip that there was nobody we would rather have had on our last voyage than him. He replied, 'You mean to entertain you?'

Back in Norfolk the poisonous fertilizer had been swept away by the winds. The grass was thick and Jimmy wondered why the ground wore more clothes in summer. One Wednesday afternoon our benefactor asked me into his oak panelled office.

'You know I asked you up to Norfolk because I wanted to arrange a film,' he said, his eyes gleaming. 'Well I have!'

Like a drowning person my whole life in my books sped before me. I saw my dear grandmother again, my donkeys in Ireland, my circus, *Anneliese* in a storm.

The devilish eyebrows now seemed endearing to me. It was so wonderful, Eve and Jimmy would be so excited.

'Not only that,' he continued. 'I want you to star in it. Here is the script.'

I took it. I felt like Ingrid Bergman. I felt like Joan of Arc. I'd had dinner with Gregory Peck, now this! I opened it slowly. It was rather a thin script.

There weren't many words in it. It was full of 'Oohs' and 'Aahs'. *Right thigh on bed ... left thigh to hang off side of bed because of camera angle ... Let Carnation milk trickle from corner of left side of mouth ... Heavy breathing, rolling of eyes, then cut.* I read on growing more and more horrified.

I became more terrified than I had ever been in the storms in the Southern Ocean. Colin had had all his hopes for the future pinned on this man. I felt trapped. I wished I was back thousands of miles from land in deep ocean, where those innocent nude pictures which had started all the trouble had been taken ...

Suddenly it all slotted into place. We were near Harwich, short route to the Sin Capital of the world, Amsterdam. That was why he was so rich. That was why he only worked on Wednesday afternoons ...!

'I ... I don't think I have enough talent for this,' I stuttered desperately. 'Perhaps you could ask Linda Lovelace. She's more experienced in making films like this. You don't need me ...!'

'I want you in it,' he said firmly. His brown eyes seemed to be trying to hypnotize me. *'And I always get what I want!'*

We must escape, I thought. But how? Colin thought the world of him. I would never dare tell Colin about this. Colin had been building up such great hopes about our film.

I broke from the shackles of his brown eyes, begging for a little time to think this over. I felt that if I offended this man it would break Colin's heart. WHAT COULD I DO?

Back at the cottage the mental agony started again. Our patron's devilish eyes followed me everywhere. What right had he to make the fate of my whole family, their hopes and dreams and all our plans, hang on my decision? I longed to be back in the simple life of the sea, back in the storms even, the 90-foot waves.

I stood in the cottage garden long after dark each night and gazed at the moon and the friendly stars we used to navigate by and willed something, anything to happen so I wouldn't have to make this film.

Something did!

I had always heard of people writing to the agony columns for help. But little does dear Marje Proops know that she saved me from a fate worse than death. The patron one day said that he had arranged for me to go on a television panel with Marje Proops. Colin said that for the sake of family unity we should all go on the show. The patron was most upset by this rearrangement of his plan. That night I went to bed and plugged my ears as I often had as a child, while in the living room down below loud voices went on into the unfathomed depths of the night.

But really I was glad. This trivial quarrelling, a world away from what had really been worrying me, saved me.

Next day Colin started to look restless again. For three months now the only use Colin had had for our compass had been to check the 360-degree circle on BBC 2's telly face.

A few days later a taxi driver picking us up from the station late one night told us 'You smell of the sea!' Perhaps it was because we were beginning to think of it all the time.

Slowly Colin and the children began to realize there had been something missing amid all the glamour of the past months. There seemed more to life than being Barbie dolls, more to life than panel games on telly with Marje Proops, lectures, films, book promotion.

Good, bad and blurred, the fuss had all been quite fun. A good film might be made of the books, but there was no hurry. Just now we were both too young to retire from the sea. The last adventure was not a sun around which the rest of our lives could revolve. Even writing seemed a waste of time now, more so after Colin flung the Adler typewriter against the wall in a temper one day.

We were gasping for the sea, for new horizons. A new idea. The start of a new struggle was round the corner. So we said goodbye to our millionaire business manager, to the cottage, the telly, the ploughed garden with its million roots below, to the glamour. Because something doesn't last for ever doesn't mean it hasn't been good.

SEVEN

We conceived – a boat!

White sails and white tents – Mayflower Park was carrying a lot of canvas for Southampton Boat Show. A force 10 of people filled these tents and the grey cells of the sailing world gave advice and sold equipment Christopher Columbus would have been amazed to see.

'Have you heard there's a special Whitbread Multihull Race next year; four times across the Atlantic?' Francis Prout remarked from under the shiny hull of his Snowgoose catamaran design.

'Well, I saw Derek Kelsall with Chay Blyth just a few minutes ago,' said Colin. 'They were talking about tank tests for his new boat.'

'Yes, someone else added. 'It's an 80-foot trimaran and it's already under construction. It's going to be a worldbeater!'

A worldbeater? The gauntlet was down.

We had been searching for something to catch hold of our imaginations again. It had come. Our world shook. Visions of this giant trimaran filled our minds. It seemed more monstrous because we couldn't see it.

The local seas had seen a lot of us since we'd come down from Norfolk. We'd been on a fast sail with Nicky Keig in his Kelsall-designed *Three Legs of Man.* We'd watched the cockpit drainholes of Max Aitken's *Perseverance* drip gin as she leant over in a Solent breeze and had been astonished at all the three-speed muscles, coffee grinders and space age racing gear on board. But most of all we couldn't forget how our heavy little *Anneliese,* with no modern racing equipment at all, had surfed down a Southern Ocean wave so fast that once she had bump-started her port diesel engine. Cape Horn, godfather of the wind, had taught us ocean racing. A day saved in the Southern Ocean could mean a gale saved, could mean the boat saved.

Somewhere from afar I thought I could hear the gnomes of Norfolk laughing. But it wasn't very loud. And suddenly all the other boats at the show seemed like toys. We went home to ask *Anneliese*'s advice.

Her hulls were all shiny. Her engines had been beautifully serviced by Bolinders to take us all to Canada. Her halyards were waiting for energetic hands. The little winches were oiled. We could add bowsprits perhaps. But no, it was really impossible. There was really no way that her 30-foot construction could be stretched to the 40-foot minimum required for the race.

No! There could be no compromise. We had reached a crossroads in our lives again. Would we sail after all to Canada as previously planned and visit friends? Or were we really going to take up yacht racing?

All that *Anneliese* had taught us would be wasted if we didn't take up this new challenge. As we looked at our sturdy two-hulled teacher we suddenly knew she would approve. Our minds then became haunted with what sort of boat would do credit to all her teaching, and then we knew we had made our decision at the crossroads and had already turned down the new path.

Robert Frost's words in my favourite poem came back to me:

> Two roads diverged in a yellow wood ...
> And both that morning equally lay,
> In leaves no step had trodden black ...
> Oh I left the first for another day
> Yet knowing how way leads on to way
> I doubted if I should ever come back.
> ... I took the one less travelled by –
> and that has made all the difference.

Now – who was going to design *Anneliese II*?

That night I dreamed of Bernard Moitessier, whose

Joshua after sailing one and half times round the world had helped him escape to Tahiti. He was saying: 'Beware of the false gods . . . !'

But the dream was forgotten with our next breakfast and we took the train to Canvey Island in Essex, to see the Prout brothers.

When we'd first thought of getting a boat, we hadn't really known the difference between a catamaran and a Brixham trawler. When people had advised us to get a Brixham trawler we had thought it was some sort of coastal steamer. Meeting *Anneliese* had been a happy chance. Now we felt nearly as confused about what sort of racing multihull would be best. We were starting a new course of learning in the university of sailing.

Roland and Francis Prout began by designing canoes, then joined them together. They have since been responible for hundreds of thousands of happy sailing miles with their catamaran designs.

There, in their yard, were their classic, beautiful white torpedo-shaped hulls, made of tough fibreglass. These were round hulls, quite different from *Anneliese*'s. They go through the water easily and quite quickly. But they aren't planing hulls.

Anneliese's hulls were more like speedboat hulls which are flatter at the stern and don't go through the water so easily. But if they are light enough and there is enough wind power they can plane at fantastic speeds far above their waterline length speed. But perhaps where there was enough wind to plane in mid ocean the seas would be too big to go fast in? Anyway since fairly light conditions are really the norm at sea, round hulls average good speeds.

The brothers very kindly took us for a delicious lunch to clear our minds. It was especially enjoyed by Eve and Jimmy who, looking after us as usual, provided exciting obstacle courses for the waiters.

What was the right thing to do? As in the Southern Ocean there seemed no one to ask. Prout boats always did very creditably, but was that enough for *Anneliese*'s successor? Anyway the Prouts said they would do some drawings to help us.

The black spotted lettuce of Norfolk seemed a long way away now, and the only Carnation milk I was thinking about now was what we'd be taking on our next voyage.

Choosing a designer really is like choosing a husband and it has all the effect on the offspring. Piver had drowned in one of his own designs. Lowther's brother had been drowned in a Lowther design and anyway he was in Australia. Someone had been rather rude about *British Oxygen*'s creator. And *Anneliese* disapproved of James Wharram designs and concepts as being too opposite to her. Who else was there?

Anxiously we took a buffet car to Sandwich to see Derek Kelsall himself.

'I'm a great believer in foam sandwich construction,' he told us as he took a kick at the second step on the way to his office. 'Look! This is foam sandwich and it's been here for years!'

Well, he used to be a geologist before he was a boat designer and if he thinks it's better than stone it must be good! I thought. *Toria, Triple Arrow, Trifle* and *Three Legs of Man* were some of Kelsall's spectacular trimaran children.

His drawing offices were full of smart young men in front of drawing boards. He was very businesslike and also very charming and nice. The last is a quality all yacht designers seem to have in common besides yachts. He showed us a shiny black model of the hull of Chay Blyth's new boat.

'Oh yes, I have time to build you a boat too,' he assured us. Kelsall's boats were fast, but were they as kindly as *Anneliese*?

'I'll do you some drawings anyway,' he said as we left. 'Also an estimate to show your sponsor.'

'Sponsor,' I thought. *'What sponsor?'*

Up to now we had been totally preoccupied trying to find the best boat design in the world. How to pay for it hadn't really occurred to us yet. Besides in the past we may have struggled but we had paid for our own voyages.

That evening we went back to Willment's shipyard and Bill O'Brien greeted us with his pipe and his friendly Irish smile.

'Come and have a cup of coffee,' he said.

We sat in his office under the photographs of the Jumpahead and the Shamrock, the Bobcat, the Oceanic, and told him about the new project. Now a thoughtful look came on to his face. Two weeks and a million words later Colin went up to his house in the evening. He came back at two a.m. with a strange look in his eyes.

'I asked Bill O'Brien to design us a boat which could beat all the others with all their racing experience,' he said shakily. 'And he's come up with a 70-foot ocean racing catamaran!'

A giant Jumpahead looked out of the careful, intricate, aircraft-like drawings Bill had done. We laid them out in *Anneliese*'s main cabin on the table where Jimmy had been born.

This was it! It was *Anneliese*'s big sister. The ghost of the small tin globe which we had been looking at when we'd first spotted Cape Horn and decided that the Oceanic *Anneliese* should be the first catamaran ever to go round it, was in front of us again.

EIGHT

James Bum 003½!

If an adventure can be contained between two glossy covers, this was it!

'Portsmouth to Key West in Florida,' purred the multihull race brochure. This was on the difficult side of the winds. 'Whoever designed this course can't have liked multihulls much,' muttered Colin. These were prophetic words. The second leg was Key West to Freetown in West Africa, Freetown to Rio de Janeiro and then back up the globe to Portsmouth again ...

18,000 miles of difficult ocean; a million mental miles of more difficult preparation first lay ahead. Just now the starting flag was nearly a year away. The calendar lyingly told us there was plenty enough time. A lot had to be done!

Although we had hoped that Bill O'Brien would drop everything and with his expert team build the catamaran for us, he explained that although he would supervise the 70-footer's construction, he wouldn't be able to give up making his bread and butter cruising catamarans. His ethics were, that one customer was as important as the next, and some customers had been waiting for their Oceanics for nearly a year.

We were glad the beloved Oceanic was doing well again. We knew Bill had been through financial storms, but somehow, it was *Anneliese II*'s first disappointment just the same. Now we had to find her a sponsor, though we hadn't the faintest idea how. We also had to find a building team for Bill to supervise. The last depended on the first. The first on the last.

Not many children have had their portraits painted

before they are born. Artist James Leech, who had illustrated *Children of Cape Horn* for the Reader's Digest, borrowed Bill's drawings and from them, in his tiny attic in Monmouth Street, produced a beautiful painting of our future 70-footer. It was a painting which was to keep us going through more troubles and storms than Cape Horn has known in a hundred years, though not ever wet ones.

When Bill O'Brien had built his first ever catamaran by nailing two pig troughs together and floating them on his father's farmyard pond in Carlow, his only reward had been a hiding. That the new monster boat would repay him better than that, depended on us finding a sponsor.

Bill's design battened on the riches of his twenty-five years' experience. In the RAF he had been an aircraft engineer and a bit of the aeroplane lived in the heart of all his boats. He believed in light, rigid monocock construction for racing catamarans. *Anneliese II*'s vital statistics were to be 70-foot over all by 30-foot, 68-foot waterline length. She would have hulls of the family of all Bill's boats, with plenty of displacement, but a bit slimmer than the others with a sharp cutting edge for slicing through the water at the bows.

Bill had organized the first ever catamaran race in England and with his 18-foot Jumpahead had competed in it and won. She was an excellent sea boat; more of an 18-foot yacht really. She had only retired from being a dinghy when the very light flimsy catamaran dinghies were designed. They were just capable of performing in the enclosed sheltered waters, which were the only places their races were ever held. The Jumpahead was virtually a quarter-scale model of our 70-footer.

On Fireworks Night we were dragged away from poring over the plans by Max Aitken, whom we'd met at the Boat Show, so that we could watch a firework display from his famous telescoped windows. But we didn't watch the sky for long. Soon Max was grasping Colin and me by the arms and steering us into another room.

'Please talk to Mr Heath. He's lonely!'

In the crowded room of people, Ted Heath was sitting alone. Maybe he was left alone because he looked so thoughtful. Maybe it was because he had just been made Prime Minister. We sat one of us on each side of him and tried several subjects till finally, at the mention of sailing his brain unmoored from Westminster and the country's troubles. Half an hour later he was still instructing us on the finer points of helmsmanship.

Afterwards we got a lift back to Southampton in a speed boat. We clung on as the boat surfed up to 25 knots, gripping the stanchions with the uneasy feeling that our new boat might travel faster than this – under sail!

'Maybe she won't be a yacht at all,' I thought breathlessly, 'but a sailing aeroplane!'

We had read that it had taken Christopher Columbus eight years to get his sponsorship and in the end, after all the fuss, he had died lonely and broken in a debtor's jail in Spain.

The first people to bless the spirit of *Anneliese II* were John and Mary Hayley Bell Mills. We found her making honey sandwiches between acts of *The Good Companions* in the Haymarket Theatre, London. They had done well and been happy, they explained, because they had stayed together. Even when he had gone to the wilds on location, John's family had always gone with him. It had cost a lot, he said. But it would have cost more to have left them behind.

I wondered if the same would happen to us. And whether if we stayed together we would end up better than poor Christopher Columbus. But there are always too many bends on the way to see the end of the road.

We had put our hearts round Cape Horn long before *Anneliese* got there under sail. It had never occurred to us to give up, or that we might not make it. Now it never occurred to us that we might have any difficulty finding sponsorship; or that the laws of the sea might be kindlier to strangers than the laws of the land.

'Why don't you go to Geneva to see them,' said the

English representative of a Swiss firm. 'You were born in Switzerland after all.'

Well, the best foam for foam sandwich was made in Switzerland too. We did three lectures till our voices minted the money for the fare. Eve stayed with some friends. James Mario (Jimmy) and a photograph of the painting of our expected two-hulled child came with us. My heart was thumping louder than the engines as the plane touched down in Switzerland. We were on the brink of our first expedition into the sponsorship jungle.

'WELCOME COLIN AND ROSIE SWALE' said the board in reception with efficient Swiss courtesy, but these polite people didn't welcome our ideas as warmly as they did us. They told us that they had already put some money into a boat for an Atlantic race the previous year. Had we heard of it?

No! we had to admit. But how could they possibly compare our boat with any other boat in the world?

'Anyway,' the managing director explained after coffee and croissants, 'the company is owned by an American businessman and he makes all the decisions.'

Well we couldn't go to New York just now to see him, could we? They turned the project down with a charm which said they thought more of us than of our new boat.

Had they really not liked our ideas? Had they not been able to afford it? Had it not been their decision? Or had we not presented it right?

We never knew the answers. We were perhaps still pulling up sails in our mud berth when it came to getting sponsorship. But this time there was no Bill O'Brien standing with his pipe on the jetty telling us what to do! Sailing round Cape Horn we had depended only on ourselves, but getting sponsorship depended on many other people, and economic recessions floated like icebergs on our route.

Looking again at the few bits of paper which was all our new boat consisted of at the moment, I felt for the first time an uneasy foreboding of difficulties to come. We, to whom a fiver was usually a lot of money, now needed several fortunes. Our competitors' boats were costing £250,000 and more.

We passed the lake, arms lengthening above the handles of the suitcases we had unwisely brought; passed the famous fountain now turned off for the winter; passed the curvy descendants of Landy, the pet swan I used to feed as a child. At last we got to the back streets where you don't have to pay for a view.

One little hotel was called Hotel la Fontaine instead of having a view of it. A 'Vacances' sign hung crookedly on the door. It looked as if our purses could stay there for a night or two anyway.

Next day arrived with Swiss promptness. What were we to do now? The edges of the boat's photograph luffed in Colin's briefcase. We were now in a strange business world, and we didn't have any charts. We might even sail off the edge!

'ROLEX' said a sign near the skyline.

'Let's go in and see them,' suggested Colin.

We went over the river, over three roads, past a rink where people in skates and endless scarves were playing ice hockey and in through doors which slid aside so quickly to usher you in that you couldn't change your mind. Then we were there. All at once we remembered that we hadn't thought of what to say or who to see.

Inside was a vast reception hall. You could almost see the curvature of the horizon across the polished acres.

'We would like to see the chairman please,' we said. Our voices echoed back to us from afar. The charming receptionist wiped Jimmy's face with a lace handkerchief and gave him a green biro with Rolex printed on it. She seemed to be playing for time to think.

'I really don't know if Monsieur Van Gessel can see you,' she said at last. 'Perhaps if you had come earlier . . .' Her polite kindness nearly hid the fact that spur of the moment visitors never saw the chairman or managing director. It was then that we noticed that Jimmy had completely disappeared.

'Is this your charming little boy?' a deep voice came

round the corner a few minutes later. The voice was followed by a tall distinguished man with Jimmy in his arms.

'Oh Monsieur Van Gessel,' the receptionist began, surprised, 'Monsieur et Madame Swale ...'

'C'est bien. Come in,' he said showing us in through a fine oak carved door. 'I admire sailing people. I shall give you two friends who will never leave your wrists and will travel with you everywhere.'

When things got really bad in the future we would always look at the beautiful Rolexes on our wrists and feel cheered up. Strange, I thought – it was our three-year-old son who had got us our first sponsorship!

NINE

On board with five million readers

'Please leave the building or we'll set the Police on you!' the doorman shouted.

We had been looking forward to visiting the Nestlé Company. We had done some promotion for them on the first voyage. *Children of Cape Horn* had a photograph in it of Jimmy on his first birthday standing smiling in the cockpit beside a tin of Milo; and Colin had eaten 293 bars of their chocolate crossing the Atlantic.

But the doorman's sour scowl didn't match the sweet chocolate at all. No, we hadn't come to the wrong place. The giant 'NESTLÉ' name poked the clouds at the top of the enormous building.

'You cannot see the chairman. Not the chairman himself. *Impossible, non, non!*'

Soothingly we explained again that we wished to thank him and give him a present of the book. At last, reluctantly, he picked up the telephone. The voice of the chairman's secretary grated in the telephone receiver. She sounded as if she was in the middle of a typing error.

'*Impossible, impossible,*' she snapped. '*Absolument Non, Non, Non ...*'

We left, bewildered. The light at the top of the building was probably where the unfortunate chairman was sitting, lonely and bored in his office, screened from the soundproofed thousands beneath him. He was probably wishing something would happen to amuse him.

Our nerve was still shaken as airborne again on the way home to England we watched the sharp peaks of the Alps become padded in soft cloud.

'The captain would like to see you on the flight deck,'

a pretty air hostess told us, her high altitude cheekbones glinting. Soon we were gazing entranced at all the dials and switches up on the 'bridge'. Suddenly Jimmy emerged from under a seat.

'Look, Mummy, look,' he said, beaming. 'I've pulled this!'

France crouched somewhere thousands of feet below.

'MY GOD!' gasped the co-pilot. 'He's letting down the undercarriage!'

'No wonder,' I thought as we weaved our way back aft to our seats, 'no wonder they have seatbelts for passengers like us!'

The airport terminus bus fare had gone up another 10p and people fresh from the clouds of seven oceans now sat side by side and fumbled in their wallets.

Safe back on board *Anneliese,* the prize Rolex glittered against Colin's wrist as he listened to yet another sleepy Sunday time signal. It was lovely. But *Anneliese* was disappointed that we hadn't yet managed to raise any finance for her big sister.

'You'll have to do better than this,' she seemed to say to us.

A little later that day we found one last *Sunday Times* leaning against a stack of *News of the Worlds* in the local newsagents. As we picked it up and handed over the 22p – we didn't realize we had just paid our fare round the world again!

'The *QE2* is going on a world maiden voyage starting at the beginning of January,' read Colin, looking at an advertisement on the third page.

'Perhaps we can go on it and earn some money for *Anneliese II,*' we exclaimed simultaneously.

We licked our last stamp. A week later a letter arrived back from Cunard saying that they were sending two of their representatives to attend a lecture we were giving in Guildford next Saturday.

My vocal chords had been saving their finest joke since our last voyage. I got laryngitis! I husked my way through a speech which my blue catsuit did its best to amplify with body language, and *Anneliese* sailed again on a blurred screen to the sound of the electronic Bach tape which had kept us going through so many wild watches in the Southern Ocean. Luckily the audience were kind and translated it all as some interesting new lecture gimmick and reserved their tomatoes for the next breakfast. Colin kept everyone's attention by turning each question afterwards into a lecture of its own.

'The Duke and Duchess of Bedford are lecturing on the second leg of the voyage,' the Cunard representatives told us afterwards. 'Ludovic Kennedy and Moira Shearer the third. You can choose the first or last leg.' Exotic food, blue seas were extended with their handshakes. But to their surprise our faces fell.

'Oh,' said Colin. 'But we want to go the whole way round. We wish to compare sailing around the world in a tiny sailing boat with steaming round it in an enormous luxury liner.'

'You don't understand,' they explained patiently. 'The films on board are changed every night. Even the lecturers have to be changed sometimes. The passengers like variety!' Our hopes were free falling without any parachute. 'Of course,' the Cunard people added, 'you could go the rest of the way as paying passengers ...'

I saw an idea glinting in Colin's eyes.

Ten days later we'd celebrated Christmas with Colin's dad in Halifax. The children had had a riot. Colin had fallen in love with a black mare called Bess and we'd given each other hairdriers each hoping the other one could use it. Now the bowline of another Boat Show looped around London; and the circle of the world still hung in a question mark for us.

It was January 2nd, two days to the departure of the *QE2* on her world maiden voyage. We rushed to London. From the station we made a wild dash for a taxi carrying our huge oil painting of the boat. We hoped it would clinch the deal with the editor of *The Sunday Mirror*.

'Hello, hello,' said a policeman, badges gleaming. 'Where did you get that from?'

We muttered incoherent French and just escaped being arrested. But the policeman shrugged as if he was still certain we had stolen the painting; but thanks to our bad English, couldn't prove it in time to get home to his tea.

At last we arrived. Fleet Street as usual was flowing with red wine and news. *The Sunday Mirror* tributary near Holborn usually ran sluggishly on Tuesday. But now the editor's words buffeted against the sleek walls of his office. We sat and listened to his word storm with reefed down ears.

'You are both remarkable people,' he kept saying over and over again. 'But what you want from me is really impossible.' At last the low was over and his voice changed back to his normal cheerfulness.

'I tell you what,' he said as the wine glasses came out at last. 'I will commission you to write about the *QE2* round the world voyage.

Maybe we could convert five million *Sunday Mirror* readers into *QE2* passengers. Maybe *The Sunday Mirror* was the only paper that could afford our fare.

At last, contracts bound with plenty of magical green legal string flew to and from the solicitors. At last we were definitely going: all of us! With one and a quarter days to spare!

We felt that *Anneliese II* still in her spirit world was smiling at us. And the ghosts of all the fine boats of the past were amused because Jimmy would be twice around the world before he was four years old.

The friendly girl at the BOAC vaccination centre scattered her queues for us and gave us enthusiastic jabs of everything. 'Have the smallpox on me,' she exclaimed brightly. 'And the typhoid ... and the cholera ...' At last we had to beg her to stop.

We arrived back late that night to the oozing mud of Willment's shipyard. The great dusty attic above Bill O'Brien's shed in Woolston, Southampton, where we kept our belongings, was completely dark. None of the lights was working. Clarence and Oedipus, shipyard descendants of our two cats, looked on calmly with eyes that could see in the dark.

As we fumbled for our few possessions and waded out in the mud to wash our hair under the pump before daybreak, I wondered how many prospective *QE2* passengers were doing the same. The start of the round the world voyage was in just one and a half hours, but most people's trunks had probably been packed for weeks.

Suddenly I heard Colin's despairing shout: *'The vaccination certificates have gone. I can't find them anywhere.'*

We would never even be allowed on board without these. Eve had a shoe full of mud. Jimmy had lost his gun and was howling loudly. Damp matches splintered in our frozen hands.

'Hello there, ahoy!'

It was our local sailing doctor with a torch. Quickly he grabbed the children. Then, just as he hurried back from the surgery after revaccinating Eve and Jim, Colin found the original certificates. On target in the bullseye of the panic came the *Mirror* reporter and photographer and they kept wanting us to stop to pose for photographs and questions.

But quarter of an hour later we were off, wobbling feverishly down through the potholes of Hazel Road, our bicycles laden with carrier bags past retiring age, boxes and suitcases with knots instead of locks holding them together. The rubber dinghy, Colin's precious camera box, and the borrowed outboard motor, hitched a lift with the reporters. Our doctor friend followed solemnly carrying the giant painting of *Anneliese II* – about to go on her first voyage already.

We got to the docks and our ancient bicycles pedalled rustily past the gleaming Rolls-Royces which had just been delivering our 'colleagues' to the *QE2*. The giant hawsers on the bollards were being loosened. The crowd ashore were getting out their handkerchiefs.

We had just made it, in time for the most unlikely three months of our lives.

TEN

Bicycles and caviare

North Atlantic storm forecast ... Visibility deteriorating ... Same terrible decisions to make – 'Shall we have champagne or caviare?'

The waiter staggered expertly towards us with a tray of champagne glasses and little Eve and Jimmy laughed as the cork landed with a splash beside me in the heated blue of the indoor Deck 7 swimming pool. It was very hard to believe that just the day before I had been standing in the mud, trying to wash my hair under the hosepipe in the early morning dark of our Southampton shipyard!

This was the first time we were going to sea without our friend *Anneliese*. The oysters tasted nearly as delicious as those rusty tins of baked beans we used to eat on board *Anneliese*, and staying up all night gambling in the casino was almost as exciting as gambling with our lives around Cape Horn. Would our struggle for *Anneliese II* be easier or harder, I wondered, amid all this unbelievable luxury and the extra burden of trying to bring five million *Sunday Mirror* readers on a luxury world cruise for 5p each Sunday?

But the horizon was the same. It was like coming back to a familiar street where your home once stood. It was the same familiar seascape, the same Atlantic as before, the same grey January sky.

The first time we came out of our daze and realized we were actually at sea on board the 67,000-ton *QE2* instead of in our own little sailing home, was when we sat at dinner and watched the executive head chef do a 'steak flambé' beside our table. The only time there had ever been a similar smell on board *Anneliese* was when I used to burn my fingers on our gas cooker during a gale. Now spray exploded off the sides of the ship as she hurtled past surprised waves and the deckchairs slid around the vast square miles of deck waiting for fine weather. There were real waves in the swimming pools as well before they pulled the plugs out.

Up on the boat deck Eve and Jimmy were running about shrieking with laughter and we had to hold on to them really tightly to prevent them becoming airborne. The chart pinned up on the wall of the Theatre Bar showed the giant leaps of the noon fix. By the second day we were already half way across the Atlantic, travelling about five times faster than when we had sailed this ocean for the first time, in *Anneliese*. It was hard to believe that we'd now be visiting twenty-three ports in ninety-two days. We'd see New York, Florida, Rio, Cape Town, the Seychelles, Bombay, Singapore, Bali and other unspell-able spellbinding places. This was a voyage which seemed rather like taking twenty-three bites from twenty-three delicious dinners and our stomachs were rumbling!

We were shown into what we thought must be a bridal suite. It was bigger than the whole of our boat. It turned out to be one of the smallest cabins in the ship. Not only did we have this palace, there was one for the children as well. Jimmy pressed a white button and immediately as if by magic, his personal, smiling steward appeared.

The cinema was as large as many in the West End and it was actually rocking about. James Bond didn't look seasick though. The stage curtains swayed and when the credits finally rolled up onto the screen they seemed slightly blurred.

'No problem!' a cheerful American lady behind us whispered. 'I can read things that are out of focus when I take my spectacles off.'

For the next few days Colin and I staggered around the ship wide-eyed and boggling at the exotic staterooms, giant chandeliers, the restaurant with its nude statues reflected in two hundred wineglasses, the gambling dens with real silver dollars in the fruit machines. In some ways, the life on board the ship was stranger to us than that of the grass-skirted natives we had met on our last voyage.

'Would you like a drink?' a steward asked Colin.

'I feel as if I have just had one,' he replied as we swayed down the endless corridors.

The *QE2* really seemed to be organized more like a great sailing city than a ship. She had her own glittering shops, nightclubs, luxury apartments, health gymnasiums, art appreciation courses, cinema and eating places. There were three gigantic, five-star restaurants where flambé crêpe suzette, beef Wellington and Baked Alaska were prepared for the passengers by one hundred chefs. Maybe 'seasickness' was a more noble name for what some of the passengers were really suffering from when they queued at the ship's doctor's for pills.

Eve and Jimmy had dozens of showers a day in their personal cabin bathroom. They had never been so clean. And you had only to step outside your cabin for a few minutes and it was tidied up.

Salvador Dali was on board somewhere among the catacomb corridors. There was also a baby of six weeks, a lady of ninety-three and a billionairess from Yorkshire who had booked two £40,000 suites. One was just to hang her clothes in. There were many cheerful couples whose money had hibernated for many years to pay for the treat of being on board. And there was the man who had invented action replay on television. He had also come up with a toothbrush which squeezed out its own toothpaste. Another inventor on board had designed the first zipper for men's trousers. Baroness Ria shared a bar table with Hilda whose husband was a scrapmerchant and whose father owned a horse-knackering yard. The most gracious passenger of all was Xaoul the Afghan hound who had his tail shampooed each week at the Steiner Ladies' Hairdresser's.

At 7.30 one morning an enormous wave knocked four of the five stars of the Britannia restaurant out. Everywhere croissants, cornflakes, teacups and spoons found their level on the floor. Perhaps the *QE2* was taking after *Anneliese* after all. The sea was the same anyway!

The captain arranged for the wind to ease its force for his private cocktail party. But next morning, a day away from New York, it had recovered its energy again and a storm joined in with the general excitement of arriving in America.

As the Statue of Liberty appeared the screenplay of a thousand television films flashed through my mind. We went off to explore America in one and a half days.

As Colin searched in his pocket for his landing pass, the police looked as though they thought he would pull a gun on them and the strongest part of the battered yellow New York taxi we got into seemed to be the bullet proof partition between passenger and driver. Inside the cab a notice stated hopefully: 'Your driver is a morally fine person!'

Everywhere American policemen with guns as well as muscles bulging sat with their backs to the icy wind on wiry little horses with scruffy tails which would never do outside Buckingham Palace. A huge poster of an insincere-looking gentleman saying 'I will be your friend', in large print, beamed at us as we walked down a deserted street in Chinatown very early next morning. Feeling homesick for England and Southampton bags of chop suey, we went into a Chinese transport café on a corner.

'Please could you bring us something to eat?' Colin asked hopefully.

It was the first time we'd seen a Chinese restaurant mostly full of Chinese customers. Five minutes later the first Chinese breakfast we had ever eaten appeared on the table. Eggs crouching inside foam balls, chicken jigsaw puzzles, mutton triangles, sago lurking inside a large green leaf blossomed on the table. Jimmy dug into his leafy sago with a Cape Horn appetite. A waiter hovered silently by – counting. The bill arrived and we discovered he had only made us pay for what we had actually put in our mouths. He hadn't charged anything for the leftovers at the sides of the plates.

Downtown we hijacked a gleaming police car and managed to sit on the bonnet long enough to have *The Mirror* pictures taken. The movies were coming to life. We learned that New York has such tall skyscrapers because Red Indian workers had an exceptionally good sense of balance on the scaffolding; and that Philip Petit had walked a tightrope 1,300 feet up between the World Trade building towers only to fall from a 25-foot wire a few weeks later and break his leg. Looking up, Jimmy whispered, 'It would take years to get up there.'

In no time New York was all over! Back to sea again. The Dior dresses and Savile Row evening suits weren't lonely in the restaurants for lack of company, but I had to turn the same two teeshirts inside out and back to front to ring the changes.

The horizon was now a neat blue circle around the ship. But I was getting excited already about visiting the Dutch colony of Curaçao, which was three days' sailing from New York, with one port in between. It was right on the opposite tip of South America from our old friend Cape Horn.

The hardier passengers were rehearsing the deckchairs for the tropical weather to come and a gentle south-east trade wind blew away the smoke from the foot-long cigars favoured on board. The smoke curled up towards the fair weather clouds in a question mark. How were we doing? Some of the richest people in the world were on board. But we had so far hovered about on the brink of the high diving board unable to take the plunge and ask them about sponsorship. It didn't seem appropriate. It didn't seem right to ask people just because they were rich. Anyway the *Mirror* earnings were now collecting like a small puddle under *Anneliese II*'s hulls. But a lot more would be needed to float her.

One day Colin, wanting a glamorous picture for *The Mirror,* asked the pretty Q'nette girls to join us for a camera session.

'No pictures of employees in bikinis,' said the entertainments officer. We ended up with pictures in the sauna bath, drinking champagne and wearing full evening dress.

Two hours off from Fort Lauderdale, we nearly sank the *QE2*.

'Lovely water!' shouted Jimmy cheerfully.

'Oh no!' His steward arrived, turning paler than his white coat. The lavatory had blocked up. Water was flooding in a torrent out into the cabin. It turned out to be the same problem as we'd had on board *Anneliese* after 10 cent pieces as well as liquid pennies had been spent down the patient Simpson-Lawrence.

The ship sailed relentlessly on past the distant beaches of the Bahamas shimmering on the horizon. Cat Island and Crooked Island, and basking like a fossilized turtle to starboard – the outline of Cuba. Our rubber dinghy fretted in its canvas bag in the hold. On board Nicole Bedford soothed us with her special suncream and we exchanged a paperback *Rosie Darling* for a very royal-looking volume of her autobiography.

You really needed an anti-sleeping pill on the *QE2*. We found we wanted to go to the pictures every night and afterwards stay up till four a.m. listening to Ray Ellington in the Q4 nightclub. Then you could lurch around the ballrooms in the arms of Joe Loss's music. Joe told us how he'd had to hide his violin as he walked from the East End of London at the start of his musical career, to play in concerts, for fear of being laughed at. And how at nineteen he'd had to wear a collapsible top hat to performances.

The battle of the bulge was still being fought in the luxurious dining rooms of the ship. One morning after eating both kippers and sausages and worrying about which knife to use, we nearly decided to go on a five-day fast.

The sounds of the ship were full of promises. The painting of *Anneliese II* trembled on her mooring in a corner of our cabin. What adventures lay ahead for us and her?

ELEVEN

Government-sponsored harlot

❁❁❁

We had been shivering with cold as little as a week ago. Now as the sun scorched through the taxi windows, I was shivering for a different reason. The driver had swerved off the main Willemstad road on to a hard-worn dusty track.

'Where – where are you going?' I asked his closed face. All at once we were in quiet Curaçao countryside. Huge spiky cacti shaped like baseball bats leaned out from the long dry grass and little goats nibbled hopefully among the stones. Multicoloured lizards scurried out of the way as the cab speeded up.

'Where are you taking me?' I demanded, aiming my voice at the slicked black hair over his ears. The only reply was the meter clicking off as the engine roared on. All I had meant to do when I had set out in that taxi had been to go to the local airport and back to airfreight some film to London.

A few minutes later we drew up in front of a long yellow building. It looked like a hospital. But a little further along it had a strange door with amazingly proportioned naked ladies painted on the wall each side. A man shuffled out adjusting his trouser belt as he went along. Round the corner there was another X certificate fresco. Burning stones bit my feet through the thin sandals as the taxi-driver dragged me out of the car.

'This is Happy Valley,' he beamed, his voice softer than his grip on my arm. 'Here everyone enjoys themselves.'

'Look,' I said, less shakily than loud. 'I must go back now. Back to the *QE2*.' It was another world from the gold braids and glittering backless evening gowns of the last two weeks.

'But it is very nice here,' he said and his other hand, hot from the wheel, closed on mine.

'You'll have a hundred and fifty other ladies for company. You are blonde, pretty. You have no worries, no troubles. You get your own bungalow and eighty dollars each time. You see,' he added proudly, 'Happy Valley is government-sponsored.'

'A man can do it maybe twice. A good girl can do it all the time ... Ah ha ha ha ha!' The giant black Momma standing close by giggled till the sweat streamed down her face and chins. She clasped me firmly to her bulk and closely followed by my 'taxi driver' started pushing me towards the bosoms on each side of the door. The courtyard around was all silent. There were no other cars, no passers-by. Even the lizards had gone. I was trapped.

'6,000 dollars ... 8,000 ... no, 10,000.' The black Momma's lips were fat and moist. A stream of wild South American words flowed in an international tone of voice. Her hand was clammy on my left thigh as she felt it. I struggled and kicked till other hands that were so like steel they might go rusty closed over my body.

There were no jewelled necks around now.

No unsuitable sunhats.

Outside to the left shimmered the sunlit Caribbean, blue for centuries. I remembered when I had fallen overboard during our last voyage. I had been in this blue, innocent-faced water fending off sharks and barracudas, watching *Anneliese* sailing away over the horizon. At least Colin had been there to rescue me then!

I gazed bleakly out of a small courtyard window. Somewhere to the east in the shark-crowded Curaçao Bay lay the giant *QE2*. In just two hours I knew she would be weighing anchor. By nightfall she would be plunging south in deep ocean. My Rolex, lying on its white strip of wrist, ticked placidly on.

If only I'd had my bicycle I would never have needed a taxi at all. I thought of poor Colin and his despair two days before when he had learnt that his bike, which I knew he cared for more than any of those racing cars he'd once owned, had with mine been disembarked by mistake by over-zealous *QE2* staff and left languishing in New York Docks. Now it looked as though the same might happen to another member of his family. The tropical sun in the courtyard moving west across its sky playpen sunroasted my shoulders which had long ago eaten up their Ambre Solaire.

If she could have seen what happened several thousand of miles further on in Rio, the black Momma mightn't have let me go after all ...!

There was a loud ripping sound—

'Oh no!'

I fought to free my bikini bottom from the branches.

The goggling driver almost drove off the road and I nearly fell off the tree as I frantically tugged down my old skirt. I had climbed this rotten tree near the mountain road for the sake of a picture. Colin's camera had to pay for the boat's beginnings and for the next leg of the voyage, somehow.

He had just hitched up my top and skirt when the taxi full of tourists had appeared round the corner. It had slowed right down as it reached us. Some of the passengers were glancing in rather a puzzled way at their guidebooks.

'Perhaps,' observed Colin, 'photography isn't more difficult at sea after all!'

Two hours ago we'd left the humid morning rush hour of modern Rio de Janeiro and stepped on to a tiny railway train which had carried us up through what seemed like virgin jungle clinging to steep rock. At the top of the mountain we stepped out of the single-coach train into thick cloud. We had travelled from sea level to sky level. We were used to being lost at sea, but now we were lost in the clouds. We had come up to this heavenly place to see God. But he was closed.

Tantalizing glimpses of Rio kept appearing, disappearing and refocusing through the softer lenses of the clouds beneath us as we walked downwards again. The city looked as though it had been carved out of a giant beautiful quarry and then sprinkled liberally with Kew Gardens. Up here the samba-sounding cicadas were interrupted only by the battered taxis screeching their way around the hairpin corners. Just a few feet away from the crumbling tarmac, steep wild jungle clung to vertical rock face.

Colin ducked away from a strange whirring insect-like thing. 'Look, look, a humming bird.' It hovered with its delicate blue beak in a bouquet of red jungle flowers. It was so tiny. What must the babies be like?

We were in a magic place where ferns and orange lichens mountaineered up smooth rocks and there were trees straight like masts; some with creepers wound round them like wraps; others with unstowed creeping trailers. Colin crouched to take a picture of a Brazilian fly – 'Stay still you swine,' he groaned.

Colin was getting bad-tempered in the heat, but I felt so lucky to be in the open sparkling air in this beautiful place. I thought back to a week ago . . .

The brothel-keeper in Curaçao had offered me a bowl of sticky dates with a stickier leer. Somehow I had remembered my Gaelic and started off on an eighteen-verse Irish poem learned for my school certificate. They looked at me as though I were a witch, my words a spell. The black Momma had looked quite ill. The dozens of watching eyes around me rolled with horror. The girl nearby with the heaving bosoms stopped rubbing her customer's wide brown back.

I was hastily shoved back in the taxi and driven back to the *QE2*, horn honking all the way to dispel my magic. The last gangplank had just been leaving the dust of Curaçao. I had made it back. But how or why I never quite knew . . .

What looked like a large chocolate wrapping floated down the mountain towards us. 'That couldn't be litter up there,' exclaimed Colin. It was a purple butterfly the size of a saucer fluttering down from the trees.

An ant was being sailed along by the giant leaf it was carrying. Five minutes later I stood watch as Colin invented a new meaning for the word 'Precipice'!

Then we looked up and suddenly, Jesus Christ appeared on the top of the mountain. It could only have happened in the twentieth century in Rio de Janeiro. The giant statue of Cristo Redentor stood with his arms spread wide and the clouds thinning away.

'One hull of the quarter scale model of your 70-footer finished': Bill O'Brien's radio message was waiting for us as we arrived back on board.

The spray on our porthole foamed a few feet away from the spray on our painting. The real thing was getting nearer. Because of our terror and reluctance about asking rich people for financial help for the boat, the friends *Anneliese II* was now making were interesting and charming rather than wealthy. Those who gave us their support won instant promotion to Admirals. Ian Bedford became an admiral though he told us, 'The only time I have ever been out sailing, a terrifying woman told me to let the sheet fly. I let go of the nearest rope I saw – and the mast fell down.'

Another Admiral was Ray Ellington. He began his musical career at nine. His mother had bought him his first pair of drums after she'd been driven mad by him going round the house beating up the polished furniture with a fork. He had been born, he said, at 151 Kennington Road, London, next door to 153 where Charlie Chaplin was born.

Two more of *Anneliese*'s favourite Admirals were a charming, very loving couple who first came up to us to talk about a new adventure they were planning together with their children.

'Of course we're divorced,' they told us.

'Oh yes, really!'

'From each other we mean!'

'Oh . . .!'

Another charming Admiral was Commander Whitehead, the American Mr Schweppes. He said I should do all the work and just keep Colin as a 'pet husband'! He told us how an African carrying only a spear was walking down a road with his wife laden from head to foot dragging along behind. An indignant American women's libber had come up and through an interpreter demanded that the man should carry his share.

'OH NO, NO, NO!' the wife had cried enraged. 'How dare you ask my husband to carry his own belongings! How can I go to bed with a man who is tired?'

The bits of wood leaning against the walls in Bill O'Brien's shed would have been amazed to know that so many people were thinking about them!

Smiling chefs in high hats waited behind the counter of the fabulous nightly midnight buffet. And one night they left a feast of sucking pig, turkey, ham, gateaux, caviare, walking cheese, fruits and joints of beef under the legs of the slim nude marble ladies on the tables and took us down for an escorted visit to the human fuel tanks, the ocean-sized kitchens. There, saucepans as large as dinghies were crewed by 135 chefs altogether. In one corner 200 extra steaks were being grilled. In another, dressings were being prepared for a forestful of lettuces.

'350 quarts of ice cream in nine flavours are consumed every night at sea,' they told us; '3,000 pounds of meat are eaten weekly. If the ship can't dock at the next port for any reason, there are facilities for 200 tons of stores to be dropped from the sky by helicopter.' 700 pounds of Iceberg lettuces, 400 pounds of caviare, 3,500 melons, 200 pounds of crayfish packed in cotton wool – quite a shopping list!

TWELVE

The love of a future love

The luxuries of the *QE2*'s kitchens could have been moondust to the people we visited next. We'd sailed from the hot African sun to the hot Indian sun in just five days.

The king cobra, his shiny, bulging, scaly head arching up into striking position, was sticking his forked tongue in and out two inches from my face. His friend, an enormous boa constrictor, slid in an affectionate hug around my neck then wrapped endless psychedelic coils round and round my whole body, till his tail was tickling shamelessly somewhere between my legs. I can see why people have dreams about snakes, I thought.

Somewhere nearby, a riki tiki tavi mongoose was peeping out from under his blanket. The pavements became dark now, as a sudden crowd gathered round. Not far off, the funnels of the *QE2* and the Bridge deck with its satellite navigation aerials were glistening among the ancient domes and arches of Bombay. The luxury liner dominated the harbour like a space ship. And really it did seem as impossible for any of those Indian street people to sail anywhere on board her, as to go to Mars.

The snakes hissed us goodbye as, for the price of one rupee, a man with his turban coiled as neatly as the snakes persuaded them back into their baskets.

We walked along streets where the poverty and beauty of India lived side by side; past filth and smells and neglect and carefully made glittering bracelets; past women with beautiful Miss World eyes, who smiled as they looked up from washing their clothes in the gutter; past a man with just stumps for arms, who offered us a lovely golden signet ring . . .

I saw Colin shaking his head on the edge of tears, trying to photograph a little girl of about eight with a thin naked baby of about a year old. She was carrying it around just like a wrinkled rag doll.

'Look, look!' she said almost proudly. 'Baby ... *blind*.'

Two rupees – ten pence. Her face lit up.

Just then a man came up with two little birds on a stick. They hopped happily on to Colin's fingers and sat very closely side by side. Then he noticed – one of the little birds was blind too.

'My shop! Look ... look ... look. Come and see.'

Everyone was touching us, reaching out, pleading, crowding round. Then we suddenly realized that the only thing most of these street people were offering was dreadful deformities of their bodies: fearful eye diseases; lives and ribs bare of almost everything.

A man with shrivelled arms and legs shuffled up hopefully. Colin gave him the birthday cake we'd smuggled ashore. He smiled as he took it. We had planted some bread rolls and sugar lumps on top, as well as the candle. Just than a young mother came up with a tiny crying baby. '*Hungry*,' she said, putting her hands to her mouth. Had we given the cake to the wrong person after all?

A little boy with tousled hair, an impish grin and a desperately wall eye came running up. He kept plucking gently and persistently at Colin's shirt and then at his own bare chest. Colin tried him on ten cents. He shook his head and put his forehead on the ground in supplication. He seemed to want something very badly. Perhaps an operation. We felt very helpless. Colin put five rupees into his hand. He ran off and reappeared a few moments later wearing an orange shirt. He grinned proudly. He kept stroking Colin's shirt and then his own. Then he put his hand up to his mouth in the familiar way we were beginning to understand. He still wanted one rupee more, for something to eat.

You could see how the smallest bedsitter, and a regular job in a factory somewhere in England, must seem like a paradise to these people. I felt very proud of England, where the poorest person can have his teeth and stomach filled; where people are at least kept fit enough to keep on trying.

Robin Knox-Johnston was waiting for us when we eventually got to Bombay Yacht Club. He was framed neatly on the passage wall and we remembered that his first round the world yacht *Suhaili* had been built here. What about poor *Anneliese II*? Would she ever be finished? At the moment, like the people on the pavements in Bombay, we were just surviving. Would we ever be able to do *Anneliese II* credit?

A week and several thousands of miles later I was standing on the gangplank, half way between the *QE2* and Singapore. A young man's slanting eyes were glinting hopefully up at me.

'You have a pretty face,' he whispered, contradicting what the mirror had told my black circles. 'Take me in your cabin to Hong Kong.'

'Well ... Er ...' I looked around. Libras can never say no. *QE2* officers of the watch were busy assisting passengers on and off the ship. They didn't seem to notice this strange restless young man who had arrived with his basket full of personal possessions.

There were decorations everywhere ashore, both to celebrate the one day stay in Singapore of the *QE2* and the Chinese New Year, which goes on for a fortnight. 'HAPPY NEW YEAR' or 'KONG KEE FATT CHOY' the banners streamed. The young man still looked at me expectantly. What was I to do?

All at once a tiny Chinese grannie appeared at the foot of the gangplank. She manoeuvred her way deftly past the saris of the 'privileged visitors' being escorted on board and through the maze of legs of disembarking passengers. Then with an inscrutable glance at me, she grabbed her grandson by the cuffs and marched him firmly off.

The next two weeks passed quicker than the boat sailed. We had now arrived at the other end of the world: Hong

Kong. We were still raising money, but I felt guilty steaming around in *QE2* luxury while our boat was still in great need.

'Protection money – he no pay!' the Chinese cab driver explained, pointing out of the window. The tightly curled up figure on the pavement close by didn't utter a sound as the two uniformed men punched and shook him.

I flung the door open. 'STOP!' I yelled.

I stuffed all the Chinese notes I had into the victim's pocket, thinking that both he and I deserved them more. It was like a scene out of a bad film. They looked quite pleased at the 'monee', but they would rather have gone on thumping. However, when the old man unrolled himself slowly and dragged himself off towards the darker edges of the buildings around, they did nothing to stop him.

It was a bad time. My mind was aching almost as much as the old man's bones, as the cab's sleazy engine slurped into action again. I was on my way back from yet another airport. But this time I had been airfreighting Colin himself. At least there hadn't been any forms to fill in and Colin hadn't needed 'urgent' writing all over him.

At a last meal together at the airport, the waiter told us of a new Chinese diet where you eat all you want, but use only one chopstick. But this time, I didn't feel very much like eating anyway. Who would have the toothbrush? Who would have the hairbrush?

Our new boat was pulling impatiently at the anchor chain of our obligations to the *Mirror* and the *QE2*. One of us had to go home to see what was happening. I was sad because it now looked as though our *Anneliese* might have to be sold to keep the new boat going. Her fibreglass, wood and sails had been more dear to us than the face of a beloved child. But now perhaps she would have to go, the first sacrifice to the vanity of our independence and false ethics. Did it really matter, we thought, where the money came from, as long as *Anneliese II* lived?

*

The strain of the voyage had told more on the human beings on board. It was hinted that at least seven of the more elderly passengers, disembarked discreetly at dead of night at various harbours, had gone on coffin launches to the ports of Heaven!

I was feeling very lonely as we got to Kyoto. But the newspaper was depending on me alone now. I felt I had to go out and get them some good stories.

'STRIPTEASE!'

Lights twinkled in English and Japanese above the stage. But the only thing I had been stripped of so far, as I was persuaded into the old Japanese theatre, was the film in my camera.

'*Hi hi*! yes, yes!' The manager insisted politely. 'It *is* necessary.'

But there weren't any geisha ladies there to interview for the *Mirror* anyway. I only saw pretty Japanese girls slowly undressing to an ancient gramophone needle. Their writhings to the slightly cracked shouts of the Rolling Stones could have been coming from Soho.

The manager kept whispering in my ear. It sounded like instructions which went something like: 'The greatest difference between getting undressed for bed and for an audience is that on stage, you must never take your shoes off!'

The sweet-faced, kimono-clad lady who had first invited me into the theatre in a way I'd felt I couldn't refuse, now patted my hands reassuringly. '*You no go away,*' she said firmly.

Then she led me on stage and bowed deeply. Two hundred Japanese businessmen, all immaculately dressed, immediately stood up and cheered. I quaked. Was it going to be like Curaçao all over again? What was it about me? What an idiot I was.

Their briefcases were soothing and respectable. But the men were all looking at me expectantly. I had no seductive underwear on to take off anyway! So I wriggled once or twice and then did an Irish dance I had learnt at school.

It seemed that my education had come to my rescue for

the second time on this round the world voyage. They all cheered again. The star of the show, now wearing little except a curly blonde wig which gave a strange look to her oriental features, looked delightedly at me as she walked in from the stage wings.

She winked a slanted eye at me and we did another Irish jig together. It would all have amused Colin, I thought. Though I didn't think he would like me to accept the job the manager was now offering me.

It was still only 11.30 in the morning. A very respectable hour for 'nightlife', but every seat had been full. The Japanese businessmen had filed into their seats as conscientiously as if they had been going to a morning business conference.

Ancient Japanese charm and politeness seemed to thrive in the modern city bustle around me as I left the theatre. Delicate little Japanese wooden houses with low doors sat happily next door to giant concrete banking corporations. Zen Buddhist temples sprawled a hundred yards away from sophisticated hi-fi shops and supermarkets. And the politeness of passers-by contrasted with the professional 'pushers in' at the doors of the trains at the railway rush hour!

Further along, businessmen unfurled black umbrellas as they walked briskly along in the drizzle. It could almost have been London, except that the banners of Japanese writing above the shops were more startling even than the Piccadilly hoardings; and that at 5 feet 9 inches tall I was a gangling giant above the heads of the crowd.

Eve and Jimmy were really delighted when they went ashore and found the grown-up people not so much bigger than themselves. James Mario immediately made for the 'over eighteen' terminal bar and sat on the bar stool eating peanuts served by a gracious lady in a kimono. 'I want some beer so I can grow a beard,' he said firmly.

The cold wind whistled down from the snow-capped mountains above the city and above the 40,000 Japanese people standing thirty deep along the terminus cheering the waving Union Jacks, as the *QE2* slipped out of harbour. It had been like bringing 960 feet of England all the way to Japan.

Under way again, adventures on board continued to keep pace with adventures ashore. The ship lurched ... The cabin door slammed shut – and there was an elderly, distinguished gentleman passenger stark naked outside in one of the luxury carpeted corridors of the *QE2*.

'Somebody's coming!' He thumped frantically at his cabin door. It was one of those which only open with a key. A few minutes ago he and his wife had been happily asleep. His wife wore a hearing aid, except in bed; and he was accustomed to sleeping without clothes on. He had woken up thirsty and had decided to go to the washbasin for a drink of water. But the door he had opened had been the one leading out of the cabin instead of to the loo!

Now he was still thirsty and the footsteps were getting closer. He had to hide. He'd slid into a sort of alcove and had thankfully lurked in the shadows. Up on the fourth deck I was feeling exhausted and longing to get to bed myself and I did something I rarely did. I pressed the lift button. UP HE WENT. The lift door slid open in front of me. There the poor gentleman was, right out of Eden's garden.

He looked so flustered. I thought he might get ill. Quickly I ripped off my best pink evening skirt and handed it over to him and he wrapped it round his legs. I had my bikini on underneath after all!

'You'll have it back tomorrow, dry-cleaned,' he stammered, recovering slightly. 'At which cabin shall I leave it?' And next day I did!

It isn't just the geisha ladies who are pleasant in Japan. When I was stranded near the airport after collecting some books flown out from England, seven kind Japanese gentlemen loaded the heavy boxes on to their heads and walked three miles with them back to the *QE2* in the rain! And the head of Ataka travel company made two minutes available during his busy working day for me to see him. He gave me £1,000 for a copy of *Rosie Darling*.

'Put it towards your new boat,' he said with a smile.

The cold of Japan was disappearing as we steamed south-east across the Pacific. Everyone was trying to recapture a suntan to reach England in. Colin's voice still warmed my pillow most evenings. But oh, something was wrong. My heart wasn't breaking at parting from him as it used to. Maybe it was our togetherness breaking instead. There was no glue of an adventure to hold us together now. Perhaps we were still one. But why then were my dreams of him mingled with the dreams of blue sparkling eyes, when his were brown, light brown hair, long brown beautiful body? Why? And why too did I feel so guilty? Arthur and I had only talked, held hands under a moon who had smiled and who would be a friend to each of us more than we were to each other. Fat chairmen with Colin present had had much more in the way of kisses. But my fingers tingled. I felt that not he but something about him was to do with my future. The love of a future love, the Pendle Hill wise voices had said ... What did it mean?

Anyway I did love Colin and whatever happened he would always have a part of me. Already I was thinking of his return at the next port and about the series of lectures we had to give from Port Everglades to Southampton. A few days later he arrived looking pale and I started remembering his face again and preparing our talks. And the Duke of Bedford remarked to give us courage, 'Let's hope the tomatoes are too ripe to hurt!'

THIRTEEN

Fantasia of sponsordom

An ocean later, a beautiful bob-tailed bunny opened the door and there three-year-old James Mario was, on his first visit to Los Angeles Playboy Club.

'Are you a playmate?' the manager asked, eyeing my teeshirt for evidence. 'No? – well anyway come into my office and tell me about yourself . . . Oh that's the boy born on a boat is he?' he exclaimed a few minutes later. 'Well, here's a celebrity Key for the youngest ever Playboy!'

The restaurant was full of men and women having their midday meal. A leggy lunch was followed by Capuccino coffee which looked like dessert, it was piled so high with whipped cream. Jimmy rushed happily from the antique popcorn machine to the electronic pin tables in the Playmate Bar. He kept winning. Perhaps he was less distracted than the other visitors by the large lit-up picture panel of former playmates on the walls nearby.

The kindly manager gave *Anneliese II* a present without even asking Hugh Hefner, also a pair of bunny ears for Eve who'd stayed on board. For the moment Jimmy wore them, perched precariously on top of his curls as he slid around on the shiny sofas in the Bunny Playroom.

'It's better than Dussyland,' he stated firmly as we said goodbye to the friendly bunnies and walked back up the Avenue of the Stars, Los Angeles.

It somehow seemed as if it was jealousy which made the ship allow us only a few hours to get to know Los Angeles before sailing relentlessly off into the ocean again. The meter gorged itself as the yellow cab raced us past the pink and white thousand-star Beverly Hills Hotel; past the multimillionaire mansions of the former film tycoons;

past the turrets and cones and spires of the Magic Castle Hotel which has exclusive, membership-only clientele and where magicians from all over the world come to stay.

At last in Hollywood itself Jimmy put a smudgy finger in the hard concrete of Judy Garland's handprint. We hurried through the Sunset Strip where the Beatles' 'Yellow Submarine' showing in one of the theatres stood out as a shining example among excitements such as 'The Academy of Sex' and 'The Institute of Oral Love' and 'Miss Pat Collins the Hip Hypnotist'! Then we drove past Renta Jungle Ltd where, I was told, you can hire a whole forest for a film, and peeped into the Hollywood cemetery where Valentino and Marilyn Monroe are buried.

Back on board again, the *QE2* circus competed well with Hollywood. During each part of the ship's twenty-four hours I met a different sort of person. There were the 'early' people you saw running around the decks at six a.m. or feverishly pedalling the bicycle in the gym and crewing Colin's rowing machine. By seven o'clock they would be drinking their 'early bird' coffee on the Quarter Deck. Then there were the morning cultural enthusiasts who regarded the ship as a floating university and learned everything from poker to yoga, from history to flower arranging.

The afternoon usually brought out the sun-lovers who measured their success in life in shades of tan.

By night came the pale gamblers, the dancers, the cinema-goers, and the night-clubbers with square miles of evening dress.

The next weeks passed in a blur of writing and lecturing and frantic efforts to keep the bank manager happy. We hardly felt we were on a luxury holiday cruise at all. We talked, lectured, filmed and wrote all day and night. My two teeshirts were worn out. So was I! Then suddenly it was all over. The Isle of Wight was in sight. There was a lump in my throat as I remembered how we had arrived back after our voyage round Cape Horn.

I felt I was about a century older now. A hundred years between me and the innocence of the sea.

'The *QE2* world trip was a success – because you went around telling everybody how nice it was!' a Cunard director told us kindly, holding a wide champagne glass – which might have been what spoke. Their battle was over. Ours had just begun.

I took the first look at our scribbled book of appointments made from mid-sea. Our boat needed a new sponsor.

'You know you are sitting on a chair warmed by Christina Onassis's bottom?' the oil company chairman I went to see chuckled. 'She just left.'

He patted my hand reassuringly and then sat down himself, peering benevolently over the silver-framed photograph of a large sloop on his desk. My heart started thumping loudly against the hopes I felt inside. This was a sailing man. Maybe he would be the one *Anneliese II* had been searching for.

Oilskins would suit him better than a smart jacket – and his feet deep in the carpet underneath his desk looked as if they longed for their seaboots. He listened kindly to my story. His mind seemed to be navigating around the blurred edges of my words.

It was an office where the carpets were softer than the chairs and outside the large windows the very tops of the city trees made another carpet below us. Thirty-two storeys up among the London clouds I felt as if he had already said the magic 'yes', and that our new two-hulled friend was already sailing around the world. He smiled kindly again and lifted his pen and my hopes as he looked down at what appeared to be a chequebook ...

All at once a red telephone on his desk rang. The grey telephone beside his elbow joined in. Then the door at the far end of an office which seemed to fade into the horizon opened. It was his personal secretary whose voice had sounded charming on the telephone even at nine o'clock in the morning. She hurried in nimbly with pretty cups of tea accompanying a thick message pad and biscuits on a tray. He frowned slightly. The faraway ocean look faded from his eyes. The moment was over. How could even the fastest and most beautiful 70-foot catamaran possibly be important – compared to which billion-dollar burrow to drill? Which side of Alaska to buy or sell?

'I'll put it to my Board and let you know,' he said absently. An enormous file and a large pile of the morning's newspapers had now appeared on his desk. Poor man, he looked tired already. A page of pink *Financial Times* now lay draped over the cheery close-reaching sloop.

'This lift must have been up and down this building more miles than ever you and Colin will sail around the world, m'dear,' the liftman joked. Down, down, down, we went. Down in hopes and height.

An hour later another of the seething population of London lifts, each of which thinks it is the only lift in the world, was carrying me up again. Soon I was treading softly along yet another carpet which looked as though it badly needed a contract with Colin's old company, Lawncare.

'I hate all boats!' the large grey man said with conviction. 'Why did you have to come and see me anyway?' The glare of the morning sun from the window behind his desk was half the glare in his eyes. 'I thought you were some friend of my daughter's and that would have been bad enough!'

I moved my chair back a bit so that I could see better. I'd have said that things were grim enough already. Till suddenly the worst happened. The handle of my bag had caught in the leg of the chair. And now it was all upset, all over the floor. It was something Colin had always said would happen sometime.

Now half-chewed carrots, an old hairbrush, my silver shoe spray, Vitamin E oil, Jimmy's toy gun and a tatty copy of T. S. Eliot's *Four Quartets* all fell out, all over a prize tigerskin carpet. Eventually I dared to glance up ...

The large man behind the desk looked smaller now that he was smiling. He had actually gone all pink and glowing. It was a complete change. He got up and moved a leather pouffe over the stain near the tiger's tail.

'A sailing intellectual,' he muttered. 'Ha, ha!' He picked up Eliot my saviour, and soothed the tattered pages: he quoted rather sadly.

"Words move, music moves
Only in time; but that which is only living
Can only die ..."

'I read English at Cambridge you know. Studied Eliot ... changed my whole life. If I hadn't been sent down for – well, er, never you mind ...' A strange look crossed his face. 'Tell you what, m'dear! Come back on Monday. I like a girl of spirit. If you can recite "Burnt Norton" to me, my favourite of the *Quartets*, and bring back some memories, I'll put £500 towards your boat – for Eliot's sake.'

He sat down a bit breathless after this speech and gave me his left cheek, like an uncle, to kiss before I left.

Is the height of a PR man's dream to make his client share front pages and hoardings with today's murderer, yesterday's arsonist – or tomorrow's brand of margarine? What do firms really mean by 'publicity'? I wondered as I ran down escalators guarded by girdled ladies and hard porn underpants, on my way to Green Park Underground Station.

Cheerful Jerry, director of London's Penthouse Club, led me among the legs of the girls and the tables. Looking back in dismay I saw that the silver shoes which I had resprayed with my special instant silver paint for the occasion had left bright silver footprints visible all the way to the door, shining even in the careful club half-light which tried to make everybody's fantasy reality and reality fantasy.

'Oh well, honey,' he smiled, 'it's going to be redecorated anyway. Look, there's someone I'd like you to meet. Dr Sam Freeman invented the pacemaker for the human heart you know.'

'Here's a remarkable young lady,' he introduced me kindly in his Penthouse voice. The handsome grey-haired man turned round and put his fork down by the side of his plate. He was much too polite to show us how little he liked being interrupted in the middle of a thoughtful lunch.

'I'll judge for myself if I may,' he replied quietly, looking at me with scalpel eyes. His hands, which had saved thousands of lives all over the world, adjusted his monocle, which immediately fell off into the soup again.

Our poor boat, helpless and half-built in her shed, was depending totally on us for her survival now, just as later we might often have to depend on her for ours. She needed life-blood of finance for which all our love wasn't a substitute. I decided to ask this splendid man for help. You have to think hard about people before you ask them to become involved in the most important things in your life. It is like taking them into your family.

'She's going to be the most beautiful boat in the world,' I enthused, showing him the boat's pin-up pictures – 'though she's really more like a sailing aeroplane.' His gaze became warmer as his lunch became colder. I was sitting opposite two virgin bread rolls and space-suited pats of butter.

'Well,' he said finally. 'Let me come to your launching party. I'll become a First Sea Lord and buy some nails and things.'

He squeezed my hand and discreetly slipped what looked like a pack of cards into my lap. They all had the Queen's head on them. It was the price of this month's insurance premium. It meant a lot. The two businessmen lunching at the next table gave us a curious glance. Well yes, my skirt did look rather short for a proper lunch guest!

I wondered how Colin was getting on at Cadbury's on the other side of London. It was just another day in the lives of beginner boat breadwinners.

But the bright sparks of the evening become the soot of

the next morning. Four weeks later, the few thousands of pounds we had managed to raise spread thinly on the giant boat's surface showed little difference. Each £1,000 had been slurped up like a 10p cup of tea in a café. Our bicycles had become a little more rusty, our clothes stretched or shrunk from endless trips to the launderette. Many people loved our boat and helped in small ways, but without enough money to finish the project they were just a responsibility.

Walking alongside the park on the way to see my fifty-sixth chairman, I saw a lady taking two lion cubs for a walk on the grass. One of them was licking the face of a sleepy-looking dachshund nearby. Perhaps this is a good omen for me, I thought hopefully. Well, it didn't seem so to start with!

A fierce face glowered out from an enormous oil painting above the receptionist's desk before my first meeting this day. I nearly ran from the hall when the same fierce face appeared around a large carved door a few minutes later and showed me into his office. Worst of all, he couldn't hear anything I said and was still glowering when I left!

What a relief it was when my next 'Cape Horn' of the morning, the chairman of Allied Breweries, was actually smiling at his desk. He offered me a sherry and a lager simultaneously, and shoved a bowl of salted peanuts towards me across the vast polished desk.

'We might be interested in your project,' he said after he'd listened patiently to what I had to say. 'I'll have to ask the only one around here who knows anything about sailing.'

What I took to be a smart office boy was ushered in. I suddenly felt very nervous.

'Oh well,' said the chairman kindly, 'we can carry on talking alone if you feel that two against one isn't fair.' The new entrant left discreetly. It was only later that I learnt that it was the managing director of the company that I had sent away.

Optimistically I was by a telephone early next morning

to find out what their decision had been. 'Wait,' said our friend and honorary project coordinator. 'Give them time. Don't be too keen!'

But three days later the whole project was in a crisis again. It was now just four months to the start of the race that was our goal in finishing the boat. And we only had one week's wages left for the builders.

A few days later we answered the phone and a cheer ran through the wire. 'We'll sponsor the boat,' said Skol – part of Allied Breweries. 'We'll put in £25,000.' It seemed a fortune. Joy clouded our knowledge that it really wasn't enough.

'We really need over £50,000 to finish the boat,' practical Colin observed to the beer company.

'£25,000 is the most we can do,' they replied as if wood and sails understood about bargaining. Well, it might be £25,000 or nothing. And it sounded a great deal of money until we realized that Chay Blyth's similar size multihull was actually costing £260,000.

We'll manage somehow, we decided, and then joy at our success took over again. A few days later we shook hands with Skol through the warnings in the air, and one of the hands passed over the sponsor's first cheque. We felt wonderful. They'd saved the boat. The boat will be called *Skol International.* We longed to go off immediately and show our gratitude by visiting a thousand pubs and telling them all to drink Skol all night.

'Treat us like family,' the chairman said. 'Call in whenever you want.' We felt a warm glow. We had got a real sponsor at last.

FOURTEEN

We stuck the pin in our rainbow bubble

The boat had magic already.

Under the new diet of sponsorship money the bare ribs of her frames filled out with plywood and glue and became sleek hulls. People had to bow down to the wood shavings to get inside these huge upside-down hulls, and came out with an almost reverent look on their faces. And it wasn't just because from inside these hulls looked a bit like the roof of the church we had been to in the Falkland Islands.

Contending with the seas was something our new catamaran still only dreamt of. But somehow *Anneliese* had given her soul and brave Cape Horn spirit to the frames of the 70-footer and already she seemed alive. But even while she was still in her attic above Bill O'Brien's shed she had to contend with the weather. It got too hot for the glue! We searched Southampton and though the yellow pages were littered with central heating companies, we couldn't find a suitable air conditioner for the shed. It really showed the Englishman's pessimism about his weather. In the end Colin had to send a taxi right up to the north of England and back to fetch a different sort of glue from Ciba-Geigy.

One morning three weeks after we had started with the Skol money, a smarter car than most braved the potholes in Hazel Road. It was the boat-loving managing director of the company. The one I had in my terrible ignorance at first thought an office boy! With his PR man and his exclamations at the boat's huge size, came crates of Skol lager for everyone.

There were yellow Skol teeshirts too for the shipwrights

and us and all elbows were up in celebration. Congratulations were scattered around thicker than today's woodshavings on the floor. It was a scene we had dreamt of when searching for golden sponsors in the cracks of the London pavements. But Colin and I felt a bit like we had when we'd reached Australia on our voyage in *Anneliese*. There was a long long way to go yet, and no chart.

By next week the bank manager's 'Good Morning' was getting shorter again. The first suspicion had begun to dawn that this project mightn't be the same as sailing round Cape Horn and that the financial weather might run off the Beaufort Scale itself. Why should we, who had never built a boat before, think we should be able to build one at a sixth of what experienced boatyards charged for yachts of a similar size?

It seemed sensible to get more sponsors to join in. But it really was turning out to be much harder than we'd thought to get additional sponsors for a boat already called *Skol International*. Yes, we had sold the name. But not really for the right price.

Should we tell Skol now? Or should we put on the best show we could for £25,000 and wait and see? We remembered that someone had once called the boat 'The sailing Concorde'. Well, it was becoming like the Concorde in more ways than one. She had to be built in the shortest time, to the very highest quality, for the very cheapest price. It was like trying to push three threads at once through the eye of a needle.

In the shed quality seemed to be the only one of the three that mattered. We felt that the great tensile strength that Cascover nylon sheathing would add to the boat's hulls would be worth the expense. It would prevent teredo worms and rot joining the crew. And if the catamaran was travelling at 25 knots and hit a log or something the sheathing might make all the difference to our survival and hers. It would be virtually a boat within a nylon boat.

'The lady must have her stockings on,' said Colin and got out the glowering chequebook again.

By next week a team of two experts who had been doing

the job since the process started eighteen years ago, were flashing resorcinol glue and incredibly tough nylon cloth around the hulls, while Colin and I, the apprentices, pinned up newspapers on their instructions, posing upside down Page Three girls to catch the drops of glue. We hoped this had strengthened the boat as much as it had weakened the budget.

Financial ammunition may have been short. But the battle to the startline was still on. The shed had shrunk and the shipwrights stood still for the first time for two weeks, as I tightened the last screw in the enormous hulls. We certainly couldn't put them together here. There wasn't room.

'This isn't a place for "joined up" boats,' Eve explained to Jimmy.

A move had to be made almost immediately. Every night now we slept on the best quality gaboon plywood in our old sleeping bags and gazed up at the ceiling of the shed and wondered whether it would collapse when we took the hulls out. They must, we thought, be the largest hulls ever built in an attic.

The day of the hulls' first journey arrived. We found we'd have to take away several of the roof supports to get them out. The shed trembled, grudging the extra space it gave us.

'That door at the end is still too small,' observed Colin quietly. 'We'll never get them out that way.'

Half an hour before the giant cranes arrived, he had cut away the whole of one side of the shed. We were almost as anxious about it now as about the precious hulls.

'Owners should go away when this is happening!' Bill O'Brien told Colin who had watched his son being born with less alarm. But we couldn't leave! The two cranes like bionic dinosaurs arrived. And we stood there shaking, clutching the camera more for support than for anything else, as one by one the enormous gleaming white hulls were poised about fifty feet in the air. We held our breaths as if that could stop the breeze they swung so nonchalantly in. At last, one by one, they touched down on the two creaking trolleys underneath.

Then, feeling more scared than at Cape Horn we took the helm for the first time and steered the aft trolley across the yard. And the hulls 'walked' to their new shed, the legs of many men pantomime-style underneath and the occasional roar of a curse flashing out. We didn't dare to take one side of the new shed down as well, though its door was still too small. But somehow Houdini's spirit and the cranes helped and we managed to get them into the giant building. We rolled the hulls over, carefully, using large tractor and car tyres as Bill O'Brien had suggested.

All at once the huge hulls were upright for the first time in their lives. They looked beautiful, like two huge speedboats side by side, in competition with each other for the last time in their lives. The trestles underneath were huge too and had cost £50 worth of wood to build and yet hardly looked strong enough. Yes, the boat had had her first adventure.

The pigeons in the rafters of the enormous shed cooed approvingly. None of the chairmen we had been to see had had an office as big as this. Jimmy got into an old dusty racing car parked near the hulls and made loud whirring noises through the engine in his mouth. For the moment the sun shone through the hole in the roof ninety feet up.

That night we left a light on in the boat while we packed our junk in the attic and moved it across to the new shed. By the time we had finished, the dust in our eyes and noses couldn't disguise the fact that the light had slipped sideways and the bulb was burning a big hole in the joist. Half an hour later, a few stiffer rusty suitcase locks, and the whole boat would have been burnt. The story would have ended already! But it didn't.

Early next morning we looked in awe at our new monster and saw a large circular black tyre mark imprinted on the port hull!

'It looks like the boat's visa for the new shed,' said

Colin. His toe had a black visa too, where he had dropped a tyre on his foot.

Next day we went to London to do the Globetrotter programme. We'd become obsessed with the new boat. We hadn't thought about anything else for months. It seemed strange to realize that there were other things going on. In fact the programme's skipper, Cliff Michelmore, hadn't even known we were building a new boat. When we told him he said that Eric Morecambe had been 'going mad' looking for us and that perhaps this was because he'd heard about it and wanted to sign on as crew!

We'd felt quite guilty leaving the boat to come to the studio. But she wasn't left out. We arrived back to find her meeting her first public notebook.

'I believe in natural justice,' said the *Sunday Mirror* reporter, stroking the hulls. 'This boat will always get natural justice. You've got to do what you think is right.'

Next Sunday the headlines about the new boat ran 'ROSIE'S BEAUTIFUL BABY!' in typical *Mirror* style. But we never forgot what that reporter had said.

The air-conditioning plant we had so badly needed in our attic had been in this new shed all the time. But we didn't need it now anyway, since the bottom half of this building was open. At high tide water lapped luringly aft of our hulls, tempting them to get ready quickly and go to sea, and little crabs scuttled around and offered their helpful services. One little crab called a large tractor tyre home. Another attached himself to the children whenever they ventured too near the water and prevented them from getting their clothes muddy.

This shed, we thought, could be the boat's final 'digs' in which she could be rigged and from which in under two months' time she could be launched in time to do her sea trials.

What optimists we were!

No one dared to go up on the flimsy roof and mend the hole ninety feet up. We slept on deck and when it rained large drops would spill into our sleeping bags. This was bad for them, but good for the boat, for we would be instantly reminded to get up and drape extra polythene sheets over the changing face of the boat's workings and wood. *The Sunday Mirror* had called her my 'beautiful baby'. She certainly got us up in the night as often as any young child.

The pigeons in the rafters went out to work at seven o'clock every morning, acting as our excellent early morning alarm clocks as they went.

The grey cells of the sailing world were gathering around our Skol girl. The dipstick of the weekly statement showed the bank account dangerously low. But the advice of boffins seemed valuable far above basins of gold. *Anneliese*'s big sister had, after all, to be the finest catamaran in the world.

John Powell, who had created the Festival of Britain's magically suspended Skylon which Colin had admired as a small boy, and more recently had built the masts for the 70-foot catamaran *British Oxygen* and *Great Britain III*, came over from Emsworth. Austin Farrar, renowned for his clever multihull sails, came down from Suffolk. We took them and Bill O'Brien out to lunch and compared their advice with that of the closer and slightly cheaper expert local sailmakers.

After three hours our jaws ached more with talking than with eating. The waitress was thinking of serving us supper too, and everyone was designing matchsticks into vector diagrams on the tablecloth. The consensus of opinion was that like the sand yachts, our sailing monster might be capable of going faster than the wind itself.

I listened with poled out ears to what all these experts were saying. Apparently a monohull with a heavy keel has a 'hull speed limitation'. Whether this is 6 knots, 10 knots or 15 knots depends on the length and the design. Waterline length is important since the hull speed is defined as the square of the length plus a third. But dinghies without keels can surf and go much faster if wind and wave ask them to, so can catamarans. In fact once they accelerate they create much of their own wind. Several boxes of matches later I finally fully understood this apparently magical wind phenomenon. Once the boat accelerates, the wind speed it has to play with goes up. By the time the real wind is blowing 20 knots and the catamaran is travelling at 15 knots there may be as much as 35 knots of wind energy for the sails. This in turn leads to more speed, and more wind and more speed ... And the faster it goes the more the wind comes round to the bows. So far from catamarans not going to windward, some of the catamaran dinghies go 10 degrees to the apparent wind. So the sails have to be very specialized. Austin Farrar had to recut all of *British Oxygen*'s sails after she wouldn't sail to windward even with Ratsey sails.

Just before the waitress finally lost her patience and almost threw a plate of bread slices at us, it became clear that a 70-foot catamaran which needs to sail upright like a dinghy can't need the same rig as a 70-foot monohull with a heavy lead keel on the bottom. There had been some hidden mistake all along in the development of a safe racing catamaran. Perhaps it was here. We knew that Bill O'Brien had never been happy with the 80-foot mast he had first envisaged for our boat. He now said that the top 20 feet of mast was just extra weight, requiring heavier fittings, rigging etc. Not only this but it could cause actual harm by twisting and causing tipping couple, digging the lee bow in. He said that he thought the boat would go better and faster with a low centre of effort to drive her along. Also because of the great acceleration it had to be easily reefable. The boat had to get on the plane and keep there without straining or becoming over-canvassed by the increase in wind power.

Two days ago we had gone to London and had spent two days totally ignoring the television thirteen storeys up in a Penta hotel room, with Colin poring over a very special kind of rig which he had invented. Yesterday, aided by a patent agent who picked his nose but offered encouraging advice, he had lodged a provisional patent.

Now, after hearing John Powell mutter about how rigging *British Oxygen* had been like putting a mast in the middle of a four-poster bed, he brought the idea out to run through the arteries of the wise brains present.

After all, there was the haunting premonition that our boat not only had to be fast. She had to be able to face any seas, under any conditions, anywhere in the world. In brief Colin's plan, as he now explained, was for a bipod mast. The first apparent advantages would be that:

1. The compression loads would be on solid hulls instead of on the beam.
2. You could have TWO MAINSAILS, one on each prong, and these could be non-symmetrical shapes. They could thus be perfect aerofoil-shaped sails, almost wings.
3. It would be a very close-winded rig. Sails could be close-sheeted all up the sides of the boat.
4. Rotating round the mast area could be a buoyancy wing leading edge. The mast itself could partly rotate too to present an area to the wind causing minimum windage.

'Hmmm,' said John Powell. 'There might be some prizes to be had from this.'

There would also be provision in this set-up to have two rollers up forward. John said that in fact two firm poles would cause less windage than lots of bits of rigging, though windage like sex appeal is hard to quantify. With the bipod mast and the roller furling headsails reefable to the exact inch of canvas the boat needed in any conditions, we would almost have a sailing gearbox.

We gave our last £1,000 in the Skol account half each to John Powell and Austin Farrar and they hurried off to start the drawings.

Bill O'Brien had a smile on his face again. There was light and enthusiasm all round. This surely was going to be the catamaran to avenge all the people drowned in unsuitable multihulls during the last years. It was going to be a super sensational Space Age boat.

But by next week the one haunting drawback it suffered from became clearer. It wasn't a £260,000 boat!

'You'll have to get old sails, old rigging, second hand winches,' said Bill Horsnell over the telephone from London. 'I know a man on the Thames who can make all your sails for just £500. It doesn't matter how; just get on the startline.'

'What!' the telephone wire jangled with unpaid phone calls. 'We can't do that to the boat!' shouted Colin in a voice to frighten away the bill itself. 'Never!'

The boat was a bit like a lover to us. It seemed like sacrilege to let her out in anything but the finest gear. Especially after all those talks with John Powell and Austin.

Next week we were invited to dinner in London by Skol. Colin's evening suit came out from its rest after the *QE2*. I wore a new bright yellow Skol teeshirt and my long pink skirt I'd once worn to Buckingham Palace.

The oak panels at Skol's pied-à-terre in St James Street were polished and the long table was a flowered thicket of silver cutlery. It seemed impolite to say that the whole project of the boat now seemed impossible for £25,000, when they were so very happy and cheerful. But an icy feeling chilled the brandy in our insides. Instead we invited them down to see the boat the following week.

They turned up at ten o'clock in best suits and neatly polished leather shoes with their wives and families whom they'd just been welcoming back at the docks after a Mediterranean cruise. They stood there sniffing the new glue; gazing at the giant hulls which we had just painted yellow to look like a Skol tin.

'You'd think someone like you would have proper yachting shoes!' the president teased the boating managing director as he staggered up the ladder. Afterwards they stood in a circle in the muddy carpark outside the shed.

No, the bank manager's message couldn't be avoided.

'Well, will you back the boat to the full now you've all seen it?' Colin asked, throwing caution to the winds ...

There was an awful silence!

'The boat really needs another £45,000 – less if we can manage it.'

The president handed the keys to his wife to open the car door. The females, apart from me, retired ominously as if from battle. Then the managing director burst into a roar of temper that drowned the pneumatic drill mending the puddles in the road. Perhaps the 'office boy' jibe of two months ago had finally hit home. I wished the dear chairman I had originally seen hadn't since retired. Colin finally lost his temper too and they stood in the cold shouting. The wives kissed me goodbye sympathetically out of the car windows. Gradually they all disappeared.

'Come and see us anytime you like. Treat us like family.' Those words seemed a long way off now. I wished we'd understood business procedure better. Perhaps we'd behaved wrongly. 'My God,' I thought suddenly. 'We should have told them at that dinner.'

'Here's the bad news,' said the chief shipwright presenting his weekly bill and joke next Friday. This time it really was bad.

FIFTEEN

Fate takes a hand

One morning the BSC man came early in huge green wellington boots and sprayed Cuprinol all inside the boat. The awful smell which rose from the depths of the hulls seemed as discouraging to us as the woodrot. We were reminded of the Norfolk farmer: 'Don't worry if you feels sick ... it's just the poison.' Well, we were feeling sick now and not just from the smell. Those gnomes of Norfolk must have been laughing at our dealings with Skol.

For a short while longer though, the boat herself continued to distract us from her finances. The quarter-scale model nestling at the foot of the giant yellow hulls had her decks changed and altered as often as any fine lady's clothes. Every so often Bill would lift it by one corner, or pound the side with a hammer to show how strong it was.

Bill's original drawings, which we had fallen in love with more firmly than any ancient Emperor had with the portrait of a prospective bride, had had flat tops to the hulls. But now some of the shipwrights wanted round tops. They would be easier to build, they said, and also stronger and the water would slide off more easily. So would we, we thought.

Bill didn't help this controversy by giving equal votes of confidence to either. We were always a bit disappointed because he never stayed long in the big shed. But he couldn't afford to be faithful to just one of his boats be she ever so beautiful. His *Anneliese*-type Oceanics still gleamed out of the corners of his twinkling eyes.

But now storms were gathering around the giant boat, storms which had nothing to do with the weather or the building difficulties. I managed to get Coutts, who so long ago had presented me with the cutlery from their canteen which they had been replacing, now to give us an overdraft in exchange for my book royalties. I told them that it was quite safe because the book sales would go up if I drowned. I forgot that when I was so thankfully handing over the royalties, I was also handing over our personal income on which we had been living!

At least Eve and Jimmy were bouncing and thriving and doing well at school. It was lucky that children grew not by the expensive hands of shipwrights, but by magic. But even they needed purses full of a little more than love.

We managed to get clear enough to do several more television programmes. At Tyne-Tees we made a film with Kit Pedler who wrote the 'Dr Who' series. It was on 'natural sources of energy' and our co-stars were a whole class of north country school children. At Reading radio station my 'leading man' was a giant in a white and black striped woollen mask which his agent told me he always wore! He stared at me out of his mask with strange eyes. He didn't talk much. The end of one of his little fingers was missing. At a fête in Bisley a clap of thunder was the only applause for a speech we made and author Laurie Lee hurried on and rescued us with a mac and wet sandwiches, though no cider! During another talk at a girls' school, a loud bell rang in the middle of Colin's speech and half the audience filed out of the hall!

In spite of all this, the overdraft grew with less trouble than the earnings. I was feeling so low and depressed one day that I rang up Harold Wilson for advice. When I was put through to him, he sounded surprised. He probably expected to be invited to another party at the Savoy. I didn't tell him that now I was phoning him 'at my convenience' in the truest terms. For the phone was in the plush ladies' lavatory at Victoria Station. It cost 5p to get in before you even lifted the receiver. But it was the only loo in London with a phone and an armchair and a charming attendant who brought cups of tea between the pips. Harold said he was glad that he only had a rowing boat to worry about and that he couldn't really help be-

Only a rose

The Sun Newspaper

Portrait of an unborn baby by James Leech

We've made it to the top!

Sunday Mirror/Syndication International

I'm the guard and
she's my aide

On a bicycle built for two – or four
Sunday Mirror/Syndication International

Chef d'oeuvre by Tracey Stamp

Malcolm Aird

Ballet of the mice

Malcolm Aird

Felcign Finger Prinz lives

Tracey Stamp

'Twopeople' Stonesteps Saffron, who cast a spell on my life   Tracey Stamp

Lil: 'What's all this talk about injections for multiple births?'   Tracey Stamp

Three Libras
The Sun Newspaper

cause he was having difficulties himself.

Ninety miles and a few days later back in Southampton, our own telephone, which I'd considered financially disconnected, suddenly rang loudly. I tripped over a nearly full resin bucket on my way to quieten it.

'Hello,' I snapped crossly.

'This is Buckingham Palace here,' said a polite voice at the other end.

'Didn't you get anything after your voyage around the world?' Prince Philip asked a few minutes later. How kind of him to remember me – after I'd given his gold awards away last year. Hopes flared. But then I realized he probably meant letters after our name, not finance for our next boat!

One Sunday just six weeks before the multihull race, the editor of *The Sunday Mirror* came down dressed in blue denims to match his boating enthusiasm and his eyes. He had picked the one day when there was nobody working on the boat.

'You'll never get ready in time for the race!' he said. His words were like a spell.

Nobody that could help, would. We began to realize that it is not one's own abilities that stop one, but other people's faith in these abilities. It is not the storms and giant seas. It is other human beings' 'NOS'! No was a short word to have been able to block so many efforts.

I was feeling so depressed that even being invited to the Woman of the Year dinner and meeting Millicent Martin as well as a voluptuous actress who had once been found drunk in charge of a bicycle couldn't cheer me up.

'I think you've done very well raising what you have, as a private family on your first sponsorship attempt,' the chairman of the CBI spoke soothingly over the phone to me a few days later. 'Why don't you go abroad?' he went on. 'I can't even get sponsorship for my golf tournament here. Perhaps you've forgotten that you're building an unusual boat and that England is in a recession at the moment and no one can take any chances.'

The baby pigeons in the rafters of the 90-foot high roof

above our boat were now growing up, getting feathers faster than we were getting sails. Something would have to be done. We began to think beyond the English horizon again. And next week chance joined forces with us.

In fact fate actually littered the smart grey pavements near Harrods in Knightsbridge. I noticed that a foreign lady with what looked a bit like a muzzle over her face had spilt her shopping basket and seemed in great distress. Flowers, packets and velvet jewel cases were being scattered by hundreds of blind feet marching to work-day lunch. The lady looked frantic.

A huge black limousine stood nearby and she glanced anxiously towards it. But it was empty. By the time I'd finished picking up the parcels, the chauffeur had arrived looking rather abashed. The shiny car door opened and the lady smiled under her mask and gestured that I was invited to get in.

Ten minutes later I was in another country. Outside was the smart West. Inside was the far, mysterious East.

English serving girls with silver trays of tea and cakes moved around jewelled figures sitting cross-legged on the oozing carpets on the floor. About seventeen pairs of black kohled eyes peered out of seventeen beak-shaped black masks. A fat little boy of about six rolled and whimpered on a mink mat. A couple of pretty, barefaced teenage girls giggled down the gold banisters.

There had been no aeroplane flight, no passport control. But I was on another continent.

'These are Their Royal Highnesses,' an English girl interpreted. 'They have come from –' and she mentioned the name of an Arab sheikdom – 'to do their shopping.'

I tore the nude pictures out of a paperback copy of *Rosie Darling* and presented it to the chiefest looking of the royal wives, the one whose shopping I had rescued. The room was now full of half-hidden smiles and cheerful Arabic talk more difficult to understand than the cooing of the pigeons in our shed. Apart from the little boy, I noticed that there were only ladies present.

'The Sheika is very grateful and wants you to go out to

visit her country,' the English girl translated. 'She will send a message to her husband the Sheik. You can go there anytime.'

The large, sleek, high-voiced chauffeur then drove me off in the enormous black limousine again and ushered me out at Charing Cross Embankment, where I was to meet up with Colin. I was back in England again.

The taxpayers' money went up in a blaze from the flowerbeds. For once it was worth it, I thought. Colin and I spent an hour walking around the gardens, wondering what to do. Then we sat down on the grass and looked up at the shiny Savoy windows and thought about the lovely party we had once had there. A last cheque in our personal chequebook fluttered to keep the wings of the pigeons company.

We really must pay the bill, we decided, before we ran out completely. So we wrote a cheque and I walked into the Savoy. The doorman raised his hat to me. I went to the manager's office and paid. Then the stub of our chequebook looked sad as a stubble field. All around us, also sitting on the grass, were people who had the look of having nothing to do, yet not being on holiday. The creeping feeling of hopelessness dulled the bright flowers. Most of these men were down and outs and in no way were we really different from them now. We were a million light years away from the chandeliers in the Gondolier Room.

We went to sleep and woke up when the sun was setting and the footfalls of the park-keeper were getting closer. One of the disadvantages of having slept in our shed on plywood for the past three months was that the grass by comparison was gloriously soft and we just couldn't help falling asleep. The sandman invaded my dreams as well and I dreamt of the desert.

Two weeks and several lectures later we had sent Eve and Jimmy and most of our possessions to stay with friends and were standing at the Terminal Three desk at Heathrow clutching all the boat's documents and the scrappings of the fare to the Persian Gulf.

We were too immersed in what we were going to do to take our usual interest in flying. The whole flight passed like a step across a puddle. We passed via Teheran which both of us had been to separately before, and on the latter part of the journey most of the passengers prayed loudly all the time, which seemed most sensible. A young Muslim girl shook more than the old plane as it took off in the desert near Shirez on its second stop, and her screams had to be controlled by the muffling black shawls of her ancient companions.

When we got out of the plane it was so hot we thought we were standing in the jet stream of the aeroplane. But we weren't. On our last voyage we had thought so carefully about what to do in event of disaster that the life-raft wasn't going to be the end, just the next step in our adventure. This Arabian trip was really the 'life-raft' of our present project. I cared passionately that it should succeed.

Pictures of the Sheik filled every blank space on every wall in the airport. Outside stretched the endless blue salty lagoon, burning golden sand and the bones of Muslims. The sun heated even the shade near the airport to one hundred and ten degrees.

Everywhere there were Arabs in flowing white robes who looked as though they ought to be transported by Arab stallions instead of air-conditioned limousines. Dish dash head cloths hung cool and white against the gleaming dark skins.

One of the airport officials looked severely at us.

'It's Ramadan – here no one eats for a month in daylight.'

'Oh don't take any notice, he's just hungry. *Of course* it doesn't apply to visitors.'

But we weren't sure. Like learner drivers, we had assumed all the difficulties with the boat had been our own fault. It had never occurred to us that there might be a recession on in England, not just a fault in our method of getting sponsorship. And now it had never occurred to us that it might be Ramadan in the Arab world.

Swallowing our anti-climax we rang the Palace to say we had arrived. Soon a gleaming red Mercedes purred up to collect us. We had indeed made an awful mistake.

'Her Royal Highness wouldn't send messages to us to receive visitors at the beginning of Ramadan,' the messenger from the Palace said. 'Even the kitchens here are closed. She must have meant afterwards.'

Everywhere near the town, new buildings fertilized by the oil stretched upwards towards a sky unscarred by cloud. There was no answer there.

'Wait till afterwards,' the official advised kindly. But to us 'afterwards' yawned like a gaping black chasm. *What were we going to do now? Where was he taking us?*

It looked like a palace that we'd arrived at. We were shown through a long, lush corridor to a white columned room with a beautiful view of the sea and the golden sand. There was a grey telephone receiver at the corner of the enormous bed.

'Where are we?' I asked it almost reverently. It was all so different from our shed. The voice at the other end spoke English.

'This is the Hilton,' it said.

'THE HILTON! We can't afford to stay at the Hilton.' Or anywhere, I added privately to myself and thought rather longingly of our old Force 10 tent and wished we'd brought it.

'It's all right,' the voice went on. 'The Hilton belongs to His Royal Highness. You see, you cannot stay at the Palace itself during Ramadan.'

I opened the door and there was a soldier with a submachine gun walking up and down outside. Luckily he just saluted when he saw us and the iron of his face melted into a smile.

That evening a smiling youth rolled in a glittering silver table heaped with steaks and bowls of fruit and green salads the desert never dreamed of. Were we really guests?

Or would we have to pay? The water in our mouths decided.

That night we walked among sand dunes that were wave-shaped in the amber light of a round orange moon which was watching over our shed in Southampton with the same kind face as she showed us here. But what about the real waves? Really we should by now be in our oil-skins instead of in the oil lands and practising swift sail-changing instead of wandering in the desert!

Our confidence that we were really guests of the Sheik had faded by the morning and we skipped the expensive-looking breakfast menu. Anyway it was after daybreak now and we'd decided it would be rather impolite not to join in Ramadan and fast.

'And shouldn't you be walking a step behind me,' Colin said only half-joking. 'That's a custom here too!'

In the Palace courtyard a man was mixing up a sticky porridge substance thick enough to give even a Highland Scotsman indigestion.

'Oh, this is Ramadan food,' they explained. 'It's for His Royal Highness to eat in the middle of the night. It's very stamina-giving.'

The old and the new had rubbed sore shoulders after this sheikdom's oil-fired blast-off into the twentieth century. Only a few years ago, we were told, there had been nothing here. Now glossy limousines as well as mirages glimmered on new tarmac. Everything here was new except the Sheik himself, who, we heard, still loved his gazelles better than any fast car and had once had a road built around a tree to save it from being cut down. But when would we be able to see him?

'Tell me what is in your heart,' said the Palace Director looking up from his reflection on the desk-top. His long brown face and date-coloured eyes seemed to x-ray our souls. I sat demurely in the corner, the sun from the window bleaching the bluer rim where my denim skirt had been let down as fast as it could.

'We wish you kindly to arrange a short audience for us with His Highness the Sheik,' said Colin politely in a few words of virgin Arabic.

'Why is theese?'

The Rolex was ticking away minutes to the startline of the race. The boat was in desperate need. There seemed no time for small steps.

The Director looked deeply into our eyes, while shielding his, and we told him why we had come. But his expression gradually changed. The yellow prayer beads fell to one side. His small damp-looking hands rubbed closely together.

'I'll arrange this for tomorrow,' he said finally. 'Oh!' I thought, nearly cheering, 'we'll be back with the boat soon ...' But there was a strange feeling in the room and I felt his expectant gaze long after we had left. Out in the burning courtyard again I suddenly thought: 'Surely he hadn't wanted a bribe or something?'

'Her Royal Highness would like to see you!' came a message late that afternoon.

'No – not you!' said the tall Arab guard sternly to Colin. 'Men, of course, are not allowed in the Harem.'

So I alone was swooshed off in a large curtained car cooled by a north wind from a machine. I had visions of exotic Eastern beauties clad in négligées; of Arabian Nights, bosoms with jewels on them. On the way we met a young boy with deep burning eyes clad in a judo outfit.

'This is the Sheik's son,' my escort said.

The boy solemnly shook hands and then produced a paperback copy of *Rosie Darling* from deep inside the folds of his garment.

Inside there were thick carpets everywhere and two colour-television sets in each room. The chalices of juice a servant brought in for me were gold. But there were no négligées anywhere. The ladies in this harem just wore the familiar black cloaks and beak shaped batulas I was becoming used to.

'Her Royal Highness only takes hers off in bed,' the interpreter whispered reverently. She explained that the ladies who live in the Harem are never allowed out. They hadn't even been permitted to go to the opera when the whole royal family had visited Vienna. That lady in Knightsbridge must have been a real madcap, I thought. Or perhaps she wasn't real after all. The packages on the pavement seemed a century away now.

The mask that covered her face couldn't hide the bearing of the Eastern queen. The Sheika rose to greet me and held out her hand. Under her black silk robe I could see the bright chink of what could have been a Paris haute couture dress. She was such a lovely lady. I could see why the Sheik had made her his first bride.

Though she talked through her interpreter, her friendly smile spoke all languages. She bent forward and clasped a magnificent pearl necklace around my neck, all without getting it caught in my jealous hair, and put a jewelled ring on my finger. She waved me away as I thanked her and before I even mentioned the boat, I was smilingly dismissed. But it was a bit of magic at a bleak time.

But now the sands of time, if not of the desert, were running out. What was happening to our boat was extremely worrying. All work on her had stopped. And time shouldn't stand still for a racing catamaran with a deadline.

'Tomorrow you will see the Sheik,' they insisted smilingly at the Palace. Tomorrow and tomorrow and tomorrow. A golden rimmed envelope arrived for us one morning. But it was only a note from the Palace asking for our help in ordering some plants for the Sheik's garden. The order included three and a half square miles of green lawn turf, 2,000 jiffy pots, 12,000 carnations ... Having access to a fine lucid telex machine was a bit like being a sorcerer's apprentice. A few hours later the telex was thronged with cables from all sorts of famous gardening experts wanting to come out at the Palace's expense!

We wrote another letter to the Sheik. It was on airmail paper which wouldn't take up too much room in the Palace Director's wastepaper basket. It seemed that His Highness was not allowed to have his attention distracted by anything that might catch his interest, especially during Ramadan.

We kept sending home messages to the work force saying 'Hope you are managing;' meaning 'Hope you are managing without money'. Well, the sun was lovely here. Perhaps we should be more patient and wait a bit longer.

But next day came a cable which contradicted this thought and blacked out all sunlight from our minds. We opened it with sandy fingers when we got back from our daily swim on the rim of the desert.

'WORK GOING FULL AHEAD ON BOAT,' it said. 'HAVE PUT EXTRA MEN ON THE JOB.'

'They must be stopped,' Colin gasped.

'His Royal Highness will see you in three days,' came the usual evening message from the Palace. But we couldn't wait any longer. Besides, our economy return air tickets expired the next day. The match to the bridge home would be lit then if we didn't succeed – and it was a long way to hitch-hike.

'Don't you worry,' said the Palace Director soothingly as he handed us a letter. 'You don't have to actually see the Sheik. Just give this letter to our Embassy in London and everything will be arranged for the boat from that end.'

So everything was all right after all!

I felt an optimist's pure vintage joy running through my veins again. We'd been saved. Next day was 13th September, our wedding anniversary, and that seemed an achievement too. We went for a last swim and the Sheika's ring shone on my finger and its pearl seemed happy to be back in its native Arabian Gulf.

Back in the hotel in his flowing white robes and dark glasses stood a glamorous stranger. He looked like a god. His invitation to take some tea upstairs in his suite was more like one of the ten commandments.

Later, upstairs, changed into his European suit and teaching us backgammon, there was an astonishing transformation. He now looked more like a Chicago Arab gambler with diamonds and slicked back ears. With him, looking rather cheerful, was a black man who claimed to be Mohammed Ali's banker!

'Don't be fooled,' they told us. 'Don't go away. They've only given you that letter as a nice way of getting rid of you. They are not interested in your boat. Sailing boats are in the Arab's past; not in his future.'

Their voices sounded quieter because we didn't want to hear them.

'But this letter is special . . .' I began indignantly.

'Ha ha ha ha,' laughed the gambler.

Back in the peace of our white columned room, Colin and I decided that he must go home immediately and sort things out there. My job was to stay on and prove the gambler wrong.

SIXTEEN

Nightmare in the sand

The soldier with the machine gun outside my room had disappeared by the time I'd got home from waving Colin off at the airport. I put my key into the lock with the uneasy premonition that someone was waiting on the other side.

It was locked all right. But there seemed to be a chink of light, a sliver of laughter coming through. There was no one else in the long furred corridor. The other doors had their mouths shut. Like the forbidden casket I knew I shouldn't open this door. But for the same reason as the lady in the fairy story, I did.

Arms of high grade steel encircled my body in a vice. Then something, not pearls, flashed against my throat. With a shock I realized it was a small knife: a sharp one.

The knifeman's body inside the crisp white robe was as hard as his fist as he pressed against me. He bent over and the dish dash on his head fell off. And through my fear I was laughing because he looked now as though he ought to be in the back streets around Earls Court.

With a shove he pushed me on my bed. I fell against something soft, and started with a surprise I didn't know I had left. I was cushioned on the heifer breasts of a girl who had the same cowlike look in her eyes. She looked drugged. I glanced towards the side of the bed. But the telephone hung frayed and mute.

'All right, all right, beautiful girl,' he growled putting the knife away. 'We only want to look at you.' But the hand which grabbed my bottom through the carefully hotel-drycleaned cotton skirt contradicted his words. And he opened my skirt as if he was drawing the curtains.

I lay there shaking. What was the matter with me? I'd travelled all through the world on my own before and never come to harm. But perhaps now my magic which had always protected me had gone to help the boat instead. Then he turned the main light on.

My God! the room was full of Arabs. All were naked except for the gold Rolexes which flashed from their wrists. All were stripped of their usual kindly courtesy as well as of their clothes. But all except my present tormentor looked drugged and fairly quiet.

Details of the others crowded my eyes so that I didn't have to look at my Arab as I lay pinned underneath him. He lay on top of me panting and getting heavier as he ladled dollops of white ice-cream on the other girl's breasts and then licked it off. He seemed to be acting out the screenplay of the sex films he had seen in the civilization of London. He produced a black suspender belt from his pocket.

'Put theese on, darling,' he said to me.

One of the other Arabs scuttled into the corner, smiled and produced a tattered copy of *Children of Cape Horn*.

'Got theese in England,' he said jubilantly. The thumbed and stained pages with my naked pictures on were in stark contrast to the virgin printed matter.

The other Arabs were recovering. They were too drunk not to be dangerous with their knives, and not drunk enough to be harmless again. For the first time Colin really did seem far away.

The large man wiped his hands on the bedspread like a napkin and put the girl down like an empty plate. Then he reached down between my legs.

'Whisky, whisky,' I breathed as enticingly as I could into his ears. 'There are large bottles of whisky outside . . . !' Whisky during Ramadan was like gold in Arab countries!

There was a silence, a time lag. Then the man slowly raised his weight a few inches off my body. There was hope. Girls are cheaper than whisky.

He got up, unlocked the door and looked out into the corridor. I wriggled past him under his arm and fled.

The emergency stairs were cold and endless as I made my way downstairs.

The man at the hotel desk listened to my story as if I had told him there had been a few flies in my room. But at last I was escorted down a mile or so of corridor to another white columned room, another key, another telephone, a pink one this time. But the desert itself seemed safer just now. So I went out and looked at the same moon that Colin was looking at in England.

I knew from the Director's tone of voice that it was bad news and as I made my way over to the Palace next day my body shook more than it had from the fear of any of the drunken Arabs of the previous night.

'Sorry,' he said. 'We hear now that your boat is going in for a race organized by a beer company. The Arab Emirates cannot have anything to do with a boat going in for a race sponsored by a beer company.'

So, the gambler with the dark glasses had been right after all. I walked back slowly. My hopes were as shrivelled as any of the expensive lawn brought out here to die under the sun. I opened my clenched fist and found I was holding a string of yellow prayer beads.

That night the pink telephone rang. I tripped over the television cable wire in my hurry to pick it up and the set rolled over on the floor and the front fell off. It had better be worth it, I thought.

It was. But the glow of pleasure Colin's voice gave me was soured by the bad news I'd have to tell about the Palace changing its mind. But there was competition for my bad news . . . !

'The Whitbread Multihull Race has been cancelled.' Colin's voice came clearly through the wire, 'CANCELLED!' the line grew fainter. 'It's the tough financial climate in England.'

But the starting line had been our prize for getting the boat finished: our goal. All our waking moments had been directed towards it. Now I felt weak. It was as if we'd set a course to Cape Horn and when we'd almost got there, the rock had disappeared.

Somehow we'd have to get the strength to finish the boat anyway. At least there wasn't such a rush now. It was still hard to believe the race was off. But the Palace's 'no' didn't fade with the race itself, for we still had £25,000 of Skol beer money in our boat. I didn't even bother to tell Colin about the drunken Arabs.

Next day the Sheik sent his limousine for me. He said he'd understood I'd had some trouble and he wanted to take care of me. Gold necklaces hung around the creases in his chins. He handed one of them to me and it felt like a chain. Amber-coloured drinks arrived in more Midas glasses. I drank mine and it was most delicious. I had another and a very strange feeling was turning my insides to silk.

'I will give you £20,000 if you'll stay with me,' his voice came from the distance. 'Live with me for six months, love me.' He bent over.

My thin body isn't worth that much, was my first thought. But he was stroking my arm as though it were gold. Why not! I thought drowsily. Why don't I stay here?

It is the mind that is the most precious part of a human being. And people sell their minds every day, every time they go to work for somebody else. There were thousands of bodies like mine, but only one 70-foot Bill O'Brien catamaran design with the magic hulls, and surely I should do anything I could to help her. Anyway the poor old Sheik looked lonely. He gazed at me with large brown eyes that seemed wise in the half light. Without his head cloth, he didn't seem Arab at all. He looked like Socrates.

Then I remembered Socrates himself had said: 'You become good by doing good things. You become evil by doing evil things. You create your own soul.' That had been in 400 BC. By doing anything else I would be going back in progress, to before that time. But I often thought about the true ethics of the matter afterwards and wondered.

It turned out that the Sheik had the inevitable nude pictures of me on his diamond-studded desk. They had been reprinted in some Arabic magazines. My pink-faced editor in London had a lot to answer for: because normal pin-up pictures give Christian names, but never identities.

'No!' I told him, also refusing another glass of the amber-coloured drink. But he looked so sad I felt I was being as mean with my body as some people had been with their sponsorship for the boat. Anyway, I kissed his disappointed mouth and said goodbye and then walked out into the hot rainbow-coloured desert sand.

Next day the beautiful jewels in the ring the Sheika had given me sparkled for me a last time as I sold them and bought a cheap air ticket to Teheran. There was still the Shah, I thought hopefully. The Arabian Gulf could become the Persian Gulf, the Arabian cat, the Persian pussy.

Anyway Skol were holding a big business conference in Teheran. They had been part of the padlock on the Palace's purse. Perhaps they would re-sponsor the boat now.

At the airport the Sheik himself was just getting out of the royal aeroplane. Gravely he turned and extended his hand to me.

'If only you had come straight to me,' he said softly, 'and had told nobody else about your plans. I would like to have adopted your boat as a surprise for my people. But now it is too late.'

The ghost of the Palace Director's soul laughed as I stepped on the plane to Iran.

SEVENTEEN

Harlot by name – but not by nature

One and a half minutes to two, said my Rolex clinging tightly to my wrist for fear of being pawned. The lady in the voluminous black gown showed no sign at all of stopping her conversation. The receiver only changed ears. Farsi flowed freely as Hamblese does from the ladies in Lancaster and Crooks.

I thought of Colin waiting for me, standing knee deep in the mud in a grubby derelict telephone box 7,000 miles away. It was our rendezvous of voices. I *had* to get through to him at two o'clock sharp crisp GMT. My ears ached with a longing to hear his voice again.

There was a shriek behind me. A distraught Iranian mother was dragging a large protesting toddler up the dingy hotel stairs at the top of which was the only working public telephone in three hot miles. I would have to do something. England was too far to shout to! It was probably raining in Southampton.

Hastily I licked my finger and slid off my wedding puzzle ring which had come from the East itself, long ago, and handed it to the young mother. She passed me the wriggling child to hold while she examined it. He was mysteriously heavy and as damp as ground after fine spring rain. Cautiously I started to rub his back the way young James Mario had taught me to do to save the BBC from embarrassment during radio broadcasts. He gurgled in ancient Persian and started to smile, and his smile floodlit the lady in the box. She came hurrying out, cooing at him, abandoning her telephone conversation, her dark eyes gleaming. The ring and the child changed hands again and I left the two ladies in deep conversation with each other on their way down the stairs.

Ten minutes later the telephone hiccoughed its astonishment at an English voice, but let it through. *At last* I was with Colin again – sort of, anyway.

'HELLO ... HELLO ...' Voices leap-frogged down the international lines.

'Is that the Javanese Embassy ... ?'

Colin answered in our code, assuring me he was indeed the 'Javanese Ambassador!' But his voice sounded quite different. It somehow reminded me of the time he had woken me up to go on watch in the icy Southern Ocean when it had been blowing storm force 13 and *Anneliese* had been fighting for survival. Something had happened. My grip on the greasy telephone receiver tightened ...

'Our new boat's been arrested,' he said. His tone of voice tried to soothe the shock away. 'Rosie, they've put a writ on the hull. The poor boat hadn't even a mast to nail it on to. They are trying to throw us out of the shed.'

My right ear pressed bright red against the receiver as the hums and whirrs and whispers which seemed to stowaway on this international line grew louder. I tried desperately to make out what Colin was saying, even though I didn't like what it was. To hear how a bailiff had arrived completely drunk after closing down a night-club and had staggered up on to our beautiful boat and had walked up and down her sleek decks with dirty feet. I listened with more and more alarm as Colin re-enacted the scene.

'*Get off the boat,*' the bailiff had shouted drunkenly to Colin.

'You get off the boat,' Colin had answered.

'Well I'll get the police and they'll effing throw you off!' the bailiff had responded, unzipping his trousers and urinating over the side into the ancient shed dust and recent wood shavings which mingled below. In the end the most charming policemen had arrived, one of whom used to be a boat-builder. They'd brought the Squad car – to protect Colin ...

But now Colin and I clung desperately to the fragile

ends of the 7,000-mile telephone line, swamped in the awful feelings of being threatened that all this had brought on. He sounded strange, almost as though he would start singing the way he had when fighting the worst storms in the Southern Ocean. They had better watch out, I thought proudly. I knew Colin would stay and protect the boat. My job was to get some money and fast! The deadline, the urgency was on again.

All the poor boat wanted was a chance to sail free and fast across the oceans. But now it seemed sadly likely that we could lose her on legal rocks long before she ever put to sea. These financial hurricanes she was not built to survive. I felt like a mother who can't afford shoes and books for school and so lets a brilliant child down.

Now the line was getting fainter. The pips went. Colin's voice had left Iran. I was alone again.

There were a lot of wealthy people in Iran who might each have a bit of fun by sponsoring a small amount towards a boat like this. But would they? Was I capable of persuading them? People here really seemed to be more interested in buying me than any boat. Anyway, one of the most important appointments in my life had been arranged for next day. It might, I thought, just save our two hulls.

The huge Intercontinental Hotel here didn't look much different from the ones I had seen at home. Prosperous Iranian gentlemen with well-filled wallets and suits were discussing business. American visitors were having their daily trip home on the pages of *The New York Times*. Broad ladies with bright jewels tap dancing on their bosoms as they breathed placidly drank coffee placed on tiny tables which seemed out of all proportion to the enormous sinking sofas and armchairs in the foyer.

Chameleon-uniformed hoteliers trod a quiet carpet as they kept an unobtrusive eye on their charges, well satisfied, apparently, that lunchtime dollar-milking time was drawing near.

The man I most wanted to see smiled down at me, but didn't see me. The Shah's portrait was more accessible than he was. Pink painted, pastel-coloured, plastered, flowered, whitewashed, he didn't seem to mind what background he hung against. His dark strong features glowed by candlelight and the light of jewelled chandeliers, smiling with his queen and family through cobwebs and silk. He was smiling at life, death, lovemaking, quarrels, violence, birth – a hundred million smiles all at once, all over Iran. I could see him everywhere. But would he ever see me? A catamaran for the greatness of Iran? I wondered!

Anyway it had been very kind of Princess Farina to ask me to lunch. We'd first met the Shah's niece at a literary reception in London and I'd phoned her when I'd got to Iran. Now she would be waiting for me nineteen storeys up in the Penthouse Restaurant. As I made my way over to the row of glinting lifts, their mouths opening and shutting like fish, I wished that some fairy godmother would come and turn my denims into something more suitable.

All at once two dark faces and dark uniforms came up to me. They were hotel officials. They trod past the silk and diamonds and mink and gave all their attention to me. They are going to hold the lift door open especially for me, I thought dreamily. How lovely! I smiled. One took my arm. I felt like the princess I hoped to meet.

The darker man was looking at me intently. There was something very strange about it. Then suddenly the grip on my elbow tightened, and a piercing pain stabbed above my funny bone. All the stars we had ever used for navigation shot through the dark sky of my head. In a panic I realized I had been hit ... hurt.

I struggled to my feet and the stars changed into the patterns of a thousand Persian carpets. The two men had me grimly by the arms. The sheen of hotel training all gone, their eyes leered back to the edges of civilization. They were trying to drag me across the foyer. Red blood dripped from my nose on to the blue and white denims, changing them to patriotic Union Jack.

In a brighter flash of red fury my strength came back. I smiled. Condensed milk would have curdled. The two men wilted, astonished, and I put all the strength that had pulled up sails during long night watches in mid-ocean into my right arm and somehow wrenched it free. Then I hit them both twice, harder than I dared.

'You were going to the men's rooms to get money!'

'Oh no! You are quite mistaken,' I told them shakenly. My word, I thought groggily, I might as well have stayed in Arabia! I looked at the assistant hotel manager, at his moist forehead, moist eyes, moist hands now rubbing together.

'We know!' he breathed heavily. 'You are a bad woman!'

'I am not!' I shouted, furious again. I still had a copy of *Children of Cape Horn*. I had brought it as a present for the royal family.

'Look!' I gasped, 'I wrote this. This is my husband Colin. These are my children. We sailed around the world in this little boat. I was going to the Penthouse Restaurant to see the Princess. You can check it.'

A woman journalist sidled up, oozing perfume and notebooks. 'Tell me about it,' she purred. I turned away. But she started writing anyway.

An interested circle of hotel guests had gathered round. No one read *The New York Times* now. Was this the morning cabaret? Where was the music? Who was the star?

Reluctantly the manager reached out a soggy hand and lifted the receiver of the internal telephone.

'She was there waiting for you,' he affirmed unwillingly. 'But,' and he brightened visibly, 'she thought you weren't coming and now she has left ...'

Oh no! Would anything ever go right? I wondered. But worse was to come ...

That afternoon there were headlines in *The Teheran Journal*. 'ROUND THE WORLD SAILOR ROSIE SWALE MISTAKEN FOR BAD WOMAN IN TEHERAN' they shouted. A few days later they had spread to England and *The Sunday Express* and even *Private Eye* ran juicy columns.

If only I had spent the last of my money on some

demure clothes instead of greedily on food, I was sure all this would never have happened. I couldn't really blame the Iranians. But small seeds of mistakes do grow into big disasters and now I had failed everybody. I was sure the royal family would never see me now.

Next week, standing in the comfortless street outside a food shop, I was still wondering what to do. The long legs of calamity kept on running while I held my breath. And the Rolex ticked on inexorably. No, to part with it would be to part with my last friend.

'Excuse me!' The strong Iranian accent made the English word sound more compelling. It was an old-looking man, his eyes shining through my gloom. 'I was at that hotel last week,' he said.

'Yes?'

'You left this behind.' He handed me *Children of Cape Horn*. Colin in oilskins smiled up at me from the cover. On the front Jimmy playing with a bucket of seaweed off Cape Horn, hid his face from the camera.

'I am sorry for what happened to you inside the hotel.' He paused and then added: 'Please come and have a drink with me or some supper. I wish to talk to you only.'

He looked so lonely I was reminded of the old Sheik. I was broke. But I still had something to give after all. There may be some excuse for hoarding your capital. But you don't even get any interest for hoarding yourself. I could be generous with my company, at least.

'Yes,' I said, 'I would love to.'

A chill blast of air-conditioning ruffled the pages of *Children of Cape Horn* as I got into the man's car. But little Eve still grinned out from the pictures. I felt a very long way from my family.

'Would you like to make some money?' the old man asked suddenly. 'Oh no, oh no! Nothing like that' ... he added seeing my expression. 'I'm a television producer – yes really!' he said, showing me his card. 'I'm looking for a suitable English girl to appear in a cheese commercial I'm making for Iranian television. The pay is 12,000 rials a day.'

The Writ on the boat hung like a £4,000 albatross around our necks. 'Yes!' I said. 'Yes, I'll do it.'

'Good,' said the producer. 'I will collect you at seven a.m. tomorrow to take you to the studio.' He extended hope and his hand as he said goodbye.

'Cheese!' It seemed to be the director's only English word. *'Cheese ... Cheese!'*

The two other girls and I smiled and smiled and said 'cheese' till we had indigestion. But by four p.m. and Take 10, most of the cheese was in the can. I was reminded of Colin's story of the man who when told to say 'cheese' for a photograph had pulled the most awful face instead.

'But I told you to say "cheese",' said the harassed photographer.

'I was saying cheese,' the man insisted. 'I was saying "Gruyère"!'

Next day I rang Skol. But they didn't want the top of the froth on their beer disturbed by a visit from me. They were colder than any fridge-kept can of lager. I felt very sad. It was a long time now since they had said 'Please treat us as family.'

I was in Teheran in the calm eye of the hurricane. But the boat, the future, the family itself were all being battered. I quickly cabled most of the 'cheese' money back to Colin for the boat. With the rest I bought a ticket to fly.

The human cargo of the giant jumbo jet was waiting patiently to board at six a.m. the following morning. I was just thinking how the morning horizon was blocked by the bulk of the woman in front of me in the queue, when she stepped back suddenly. All the weight of her right stiletto heel crushed into the bare skin and bone of one of my unarmoured feet, clad only in Dr Scholls. I suppose it served me right for thinking rude thoughts about her.

It got worse as I hobbled on board the aircraft. But worse was the sick feeling in my stomach. The financial hurricane had screamed through our lives. What damage had it done?

EIGHTEEN

I name this ship *Francis Drake*

If I had sold my body, at least I could have done that again and again and it would still have belonged to me – more certainly than a homing pigeon. But Coutts still had my royalties, our income; I couldn't hand them over again. We had to get some money from somewhere.

The East may have been in Ramadan, the West may have been in recession, but the banks still had money. With toes still sore from the fat lady on the aeroplane I stepped on to the ferry to Guernsey where there are meant to be over three hundred banks.

Soon I was hobbling down a street where the banks grew like weeds with deep vault roots. This was a new adventure for me.

'We only deal in loans of two million and upwards,' said the Bank of Chicago, the first on my list.

'Oh!'

The Black Horse at Lloyd's gave me a blacker look for the opposite reason.

Third on my list of thirty-seven of the finest was the Nat West whose front entrance sported a barometer and wind direction indicator. The bank manager's office looked out over the harbour and I really was getting my sea legs in this financial storm because I managed to speak quite steadily. My face was on the front page of the local newspaper on his desk. But that didn't mean anything. The Queen's face on a bit of paper was worth more than mine.

'Er ... the boat needs a loan of several thousand pounds.'

'Oh yes,' said the manager. 'No problem, you can pick

up the cheque tomorrow,' and he carried on talking about sailing.

It seemed like magic. I wanted to shake him and ask again and again, 'Are you quite sure?' But luckily I didn't! I was so delighted with him I wanted to pay him back before we'd spent the loan.

'Look how well I've done the washing,' said Colin, showing me the large laundry bag he'd brought to the airport to meet me. Inside was the surprise of a gorgeous fur coat.

'Oh no!' I started. 'It's most lovely but you haven't ...'

'No, no,' he reassured me! 'I got it from *The Sun*. And it is actually new. It didn't have to last the previous owner a lifetime.' The cold of fear and apprehension and frost all disappeared. For inside the lovely coat it became summer again. Surely our problems were all over now.

But the loan was like one meal to a starving family in India. There was still trouble with the sponsor and trouble with the writ. We felt very depressed. Only the huge Skol signs which Colin had magically produced scaled up from a beer can to a giant stencil and had stencilled on the stern of the hulls went on looking cheerful and shouting 'Lager language' in the gloom of the shed, unaware of any of these troubles. Colin hadn't the heart to take them off. A giant phone bill, the legacy of my Arabian visit, took an enormous bite out of the financial meal I'd brought from Guernsey.

We felt totally homeless, totally boatless. Not so long ago we'd had so much we'd been on the crest of the wave. Now we were in the trough and millions of tons of troubled water seemed likely to bury us. We missed *Anneliese* desperately.

It was horrible being homeless in the reflection of the children's shining Christmas eyes. It was a very pure vintage of loneliness. My writing paper covered some presents for the family. But we had nowhere to go.

Christmas Eve arrived. We wished we'd still had the little plastic Christmas tree we had surprised the albatrosses with, deep in the Southern Ocean. We had stolen a Christmas then as we'd crossed the International Date Line. Maybe we'd have to give it back now.

There was just one room left at the local inn. We hung up the stockings at the end of the strange beds. Eve and Jimmy hoped Father Christmas would know where to come.

At sea, every time you shoot a fresh morning sun you're having a new start. Now we had a brand new year. Our sponsorship problems had upset us. But they couldn't dam the flow of our life.

However, I was worried about Colin and when he arranged to go up to rest in a cottage loaned by a friend of mine I was relieved. Better that I should have twice the work in trying to get sponsorship all by myself – than that I should have to worry about the weak heart Colin had always told me he had. In the end hospitals did tests and said there was nothing wrong.

But still Skye probably saved the world from knowing that this man, so smiling publicly, was really so much a slave to his nerves that he was often impossible to live with. If a stranger is cruel verbally it means nothing. But if someone you love is cruel – there is no armour of the soul against it.

Anyway, Colin took the long train to Skye where the wind howled a bit like that in the Southern Ocean and went to stay in a cottage in Tarskavaig where the chief cook was a brown rat called Ratto, who said that human beings were more useful companions than the sheep he was used to – as they left more tempting titbits around.

The following weekend I went up to see Colin. A Martian climbing on board the sleeper in grimy King's Cross would never believe he'd end up in Skye. I went to sleep to the lullaby of the station loudspeaker and woke up with a cup of tea in the middle of wild snowy mountains. A gale was howling the fins off the kippers in Mallaig as my train drew in.

'Chay Blyth capsized during sailing trials' sang a local headline. So – our great rival, the monster that had grown larger every time we'd thought of it, had capsized and our boat hadn't even been finished yet. Chay's boat had been collided with, lost half a float and capsized. I remembered how one of Bill's Oceanics had also had five foot knocked off the bow by a tanker. And how it had been afloat the right way up and able to be beached five days later in a gale. I sent Chay a telegram of condolence.

Then I spoke to Colin across the water from the harbour master's hut. Prince Charlie's bonnie boat had managed gale waves. But the present-day ferry was reluctant. The Captain refused to dock in Skye and they had to drop me into a rowing boat half way across.

The worst problem was not the rough sea, but what to do with my fur coat. I'd nowhere to keep it dry, so I kept it on and forced my raincoat on top of it. Colin's super-fat wife arrived in Skye, and in the pub a few minutes later another of Colin's wives – a thin one – appeared.

At last we had peace. Ratto scuttled around but didn't interrupt as we sat in our polar sleeping bags in the living-room armchairs of the cottage and discussed the future.

The Cuillin Hills always cheered us up when we looked at them and one morning things were even better because a charming letter and subscription towards our boat from Christopher Lee himself was waiting in the dank postbox at the bottom of our lane.

It encouraged me again, and I got out my blue appointment notebook once more and ran five miles to the nearest telephone box, to try and make more appointments with more large firms for potential sponsorship which could save the boat.

Distance really did seem to command respect: 'You say you are phoning from Skye?' the firms' secretaries would exclaim in an awed tone. 'Well – will it be convenient for you to see the chairman ...' and a speedy appointment would be arranged.

Next day Colin filled the briefcase of my mind with what to do and sent me down as his ambassador to England with three special missions.

The writ from the boatbuilders about those unpaid bills was still tormenting us and the first mission was to hand in Colin's affidavit about the fate of our boat to the lawyers. The solicitor's face competed with the gloom of his office when he saw what Colin had written to him and he threatened to change much of it. But at least it saved our poor boat from being sold for matchwood – for the time being at least.

The next task was to fetch Eve who was on half-term holiday, label her, evacuation style, and put her on the King's Cross sleeper to Skye to visit her Dad. On arrival she reported that she'd had three breakfasts and four cups of coffee.

The third task was to spray my shoes silver again. But it was very hard to be businesslike. I was a writer and a sailor. I was not a saleswoman, or a businesswoman.

Then I remembered what the Duke of Bedford had said on board the *QE2* as he'd joined our supporters' club: 'Don't worry too much about finance. Boats, I'm sure, like interesting people more than rich ones.' I thought of Christopher Lee, John Mills, Ray Ellington, Sergeant Commer, the police constable from Wimbledon, and all the other charming people who'd been promoted to Admirals. To think of them gave me a warm glow and I knew I would do anything not to let them down. Perhaps I should brave the giant companies again. Or perhaps the warm glow should spread a little. Perhaps because I felt so sad and needed encouragement even more than money, I set out to see interesting, enthusiastic people instead of rich ones.

'I've got just three minutes to the News!' Richard Baker had said, the first person ever to encourage me with my writing when I had come back from hitch-hiking to India and Russia years ago. 'I've never been so quickly convinced of anything!' he said one and a half minutes later, writing his name in my supporters' book.

I thought of other brave Admirals ...

'What?' said Batman, alias Adam West. 'A sailing Batmobile? Of course I'll support it!'

'Great, man!' said the drummer from the Hot Chocolate group.

'How wonderful,' said David Nixon, Eve's hero, when the boat gave him a photograph of herself. 'I promise to take it around with me and pin it up in my dressing rooms wherever I go! ... Jon,' he called out, and as if by magic Jon Pertwee came over to the Thames Television restaurant table where we were eating lunch together. Aside to me, magician's assistant for the first time in my life, he whispered, 'Watch his eyes when I show him the photograph of your boat!'

A bit later Jon Pertwee, minus the Dr Who telephone box, made the day of the Sea Scouts who were helping the boat by becoming the first of the boat's Admirals to come down and see her.

I felt these lovely people had joined in our adventure for its pleasures, not its problems, so we didn't tell them any of the boat's difficulties. Though we were still broke financially, we were rich in encouragement. Colin chose a telephone answering and message service in London, by voice from Skye, and our friends were able to ring up and hear any good news. But the bad news we kept concentrated in a safe inside ourselves.

We met Jimmy Young again at a BBC radio programme in Plymouth which he skippered with an efficiency which left him free to lark around and make jokes; and he told everyone on the air that he was coming on our next voyage with us!

I met Terry Wogan under the dumb-bells at Westside Health Club where it was rumoured that some lady members spent all day in the sauna bath, even bringing their sandwiches in at lunchtime.

Writer Dick Francis became an Admiral too. He was the only thriller writer we'd ever had to buy in hardback because we'd read all his other books and the suspense was too much to wait for the latest to emerge in paupers' paperback.

Two of the finest Admirals of all were Millicent Martin, our partner in crime at the Woman of the Year dinner the year before, and her husband Norman Eshley. They'd always guarantee a bed on their floor if one found oneself lost in London late at night. Midnight was just 'after work' for them.

These people were the rainbows behind the rainclouds surrounding the project. Another rainbow was the Ocean Youth Club's 71-foot ketch, *Francis Drake*. Richard Sparrow, the chairman of the Ocean Youth Club, rang up our public relations man in the Midlands and asked if he could contact us to come up there to launch her.

I was worried about having no money for any suitable clothes. In the end I bought a pretty though rather out of date miniskirt from an Oxfam shop for 5p.

The frost on the lord mayor's chain began to melt as a cold sun peeped out of its cloud mufflers. A terrier wind nipped my ankles. The conductor lifted his arm and I lifted the large, nylon-stockinged champagne bottle. For the third time the brass band on the dockside started up.

They had thought that putting the bottle in a stocking would save the splinters from flying around when it broke. If it broke! 'If the Cascover nylon sheathing around our hulls is as strong as this,' I thought, 'our catamaran really will be the strongest ever built.'

My arms ached already. But with another great thud I brought the bottle down on the bows once more. It still looked good enough to be sold off the shelves all over again! At the fourth flat F it finally burst, launching Colin as well as the *Francis Drake*, and his trousers and the bows became drunk with champagne. The stocking hadn't worked either! Five tiny ladders started down my legs where the splinters had flown.

The weekend we spent at the home of Richard Sparrow, OYC's catalyst, changed our lives in a way which had nothing to do with the sea or our project. Colin and I had gone out early one morning for a two-minute walk and a half-hour talk.

'Hello, Lovebirds,' Richard had shouted from the kitchen as we'd arrived back. 'Imagine going for a ten-mile walk at this hour of the morning!'

'They go for a ten-mile run each morning,' he told his wife later that day. By evening the rumour had spread, through a large cocktail party organized in OYC's honour. Next day we blew the dust off our plimsolls and actually did run nearly one mile. After tea with the chocolate cake and champagne still churning inside us, we managed a slightly longer run. His kindly remark had changed our lives.

We panted and puffed through the next weeks. We now had a reputation to keep up. After that things were never so bad, because however frightening the situation, our hearts couldn't beat harder than they had when propelling us up that first early morning hill!

A month later we were puffing out the words of our welcoming speeches for the arrival ceremony of *Francis Drake,* as we did our early morning run to Anglesey Lighthouse and back. The lovebird spell was still working. Our hearts were thumping now. But only with the ominous feeling that spoiled the treats surrounding any public occasion when we had to make speeches. 'Perhaps the Queen reads her speeches so that she can enjoy her dinner,' suggested Colin.

A nice Welshman had taught Colin his speech in Welsh. He practised it and then later asked another Anglesey man what some of the words meant. 'Oh sorry!' he said apologetically. 'We don't speak Welsh here.'

It was lovely to see our god-daughter *Francis Drake* again. We needn't have worried about the speeches. One of the famous fleet of OYC ketches which give so many youngsters from all walks of life their first taste of the sea, and the sea its first taste of them, she herself earned the applause of the fairly large crowd of people gathered round for the ceremony. We were just the understudies.

Afterwards we were shown through the huge factory

of Anglesey Aluminium. As we goggled at the gigantic furnaces, the complicated overhead railway systems, the giant ovens and blocks of graphite and mounds of alumina powder, we felt a new respect for *Anneliese*'s faithful main and mizzen masts.

The great factory building was carefully designed to blend in with the sky. It inspired us. If Anglesey had managed to organize a project of this size and expense, surely we'd manage to build our 70-foot catamaran. Certainly we'd have to hurry up. The baby pigeons in our giant shed had all grown up now and went to work like their parents. If only they could help with the shed rent which would be due again soon.

NINETEEN

Grievous bodily harm

My clothes were old and tatty now. Even the pavements looked grimier. Walking along the streets near Victoria, looking up at the big shiny doors of the large firms, I wondered how I should ever have the courage to go and ask a big company for sponsorship again. I felt that if I went into the shiny polished offices, the secretaries would just put me into their wastepaper baskets.

I was nobody, from nowhere. The pearl necklace the Sheika had once given me was just a mirage memory now. But I missed more the silver strand of hope.

'Hello, you're Rosie Swale aren't you?'

I looked across into a twinkling pair of wise blue eyes. They belonged to an erect old lady with stories written over the beautiful bone structure of her face. She was straight out of a poem I had once written on the train to Ireland. A little mongrel dog gambolled at her feet and wound his lead round and round my legs as well as hers.

She opened a faded purse and pressed a pound note into my hand. 'It's for the boat,' she said. 'I'd like to help.'

She was smiling and her smile made me want to cry in a way that none of our troubles had. I looked at her neatly-pressed well-worn suit. The £1 must be part of her pension. I felt I couldn't offend her by refusing and as I took it, it meant more than all the thousands of pounds from big companies who only had to write out a cheque.

She was the first person I hadn't had to ask. For once I hadn't had to screw up my courage to beg. I thanked her and couldn't keep the tears out of my eyes. She held out a long slender hand to say goodbye. Her little dog's wet nose pressed against my ankles once or twice and then she'd gone. Perhaps the silver thread of hope hadn't broken after all. It was still there. I had to make a success of the boat now, if only for her sake.

Tantalizing smells of hamburgers and coffee were coming from a nearby snackbar. The pound note was crisp in my hand. But I knew now that I could never spend it. It was a sacred trust. It was hope. It proved that there was still love in the world, still kindness. I knew now that the boat only had a chance to get finished at all if the people involved with her were chosen for their high human quality. This in the end would mean more than any £1,000,000 cheque.

I took the elderly lady's £1 down to Southampton where Colin was working on the boat and we tenderly fibreglassed it into the main beam. It would help hold the boat together. The old lady would sail around the world with us.

The little old lady seemed to be with me everywhere now, helping me. Two weeks later things were better. I still didn't have the courage to visit the large firms but I felt inspired to interest people rich in spirit in the boat anyway. Bing Crosby coming out from a Palladium performance at midnight fell in love with my bicycle as I cycled up to him through the forest of autograph books. When I told him about our dream boat, he scandalized his fans by pressing several notes into my hand.

Another splendid-looking, tall gentleman I met at a literary party and thought rather nice without even knowing who he was, insisted on becoming an Admiral too. He turned out to be Lord Longford. I didn't dare tell him that the editor of *Penthouse* was an Admiral too.

Next, Ernie Wise and Marje Proops joined the supporters' club and a large advertising company presented us with special little membership cards. These had an insignia on the side of the beautiful painting James Leech had done of our boat before she was born; the painting which had inspired us all the way around the world in the *QE2*.

I looked at the little reproduction now and felt unhappy. I didn't know why. I felt I had to go and see the artist immediately. The light in his attic studio window in Monmouth Street looked dim. The bell cried vainly for ten minutes. I gave up and flung a handful of half-pennies up at the window. I saw a shadow move inside. Somebody must be there.

Then James appeared at the door. He fumbled with the catch, closing it behind us. I looked down at his hands and got a shock. The sensitive hands that had done the beautiful painting which had spurred us on right from the beginning, were all crippled. He could hardly move them. His art was the high priesthood of manual labour. But he had gone into hospital for some simple injection, a mistake had been made and now his hands were crippled. Pioneer dust had settled on his easels. He couldn't earn his living.

I felt immensely helpless. And all our problems suddenly seemed very small beside his. His friends had said, 'Sue the hospital.' But how can you buy a new pair of hands with damages? I left sadly. But James's spirit and that of the beautiful old lady stayed with us, making us determined to fight harder than ever to get the boat finished.

The supporters' organization was growing. Westside Health Club joined after I'd run ten miles for them in aid of the Olympic Games. So did some of the London gambling clubs. If only I'd been able to confide our troubles to these kind friends perhaps the weather could have changed. But we didn't, and it didn't!

After my epic ten-mile run I went to see the London International Sporting Club. I was still muddy in my running shoes and shorts. I was made welcome with a large fresh orange juice. Over my shoulder I could see a fat man with a pile of chips in front of him. They were piled really high. Then I saw that each chip was worth £100. Oh God! Why did I find asking for money so much harder than sailing around Cape Horn?

Next week I went down for the start of the *Observer* Single Handed Transatlantic race, and looked longingly at all the beautiful masts and fittings and at the lucky people about to go to sea for several weeks and realized it is no good just having the courage to sail across oceans, you have to have the courage to deal with high finance as well. The chasm has to be filled with pound notes before you can cross it.

No wonder green is an unlucky colour for boats. Our 70-footer would have turned green without any paint if she could have seen the entrants for the OSTAR congregated at Millbay Dock. None, I thought, proudly, was any match for her potential. But they all had the masts, sails, winches, sheets, windspeed indicators and instruments that she yearned for.

The 235-foot *Club Mediterrané*, with its four great masts, filled one whole side of the dock. I learnt that she'd been launched upside down and rolled over in the water. In her cockpits were television cameras for looking at the sails. If Alain Colas, still limping badly from when he had nearly sliced his foot off in a sailing accident, could sail this giant alone across the Atlantic, surely Colin and I would be crew enough for our 70-footer.

'The crew for the Round the World Race must be over five,' stated the Whitbread Rules.

'Well,' quipped Colin, 'Jimmy is five now and Eve seven.'

How the years had fled! Thank God Eve and Jimmy were happy and knew nothing of all our financial traumas. Their biggest financial worry was counting up their pennies for the Saturday morning pictures.

'You'd think,' said Alain Colas, 'that with all this big yacht and everything I would be rich. The truth is I have nothing at all.' Perhaps we weren't so different after all!

We missed the start itself because we had to dash up to the Midlands to do one of the lectures that were our only source of personal income. The words out of our mouths put the bread into our mouths.

Travelling by train was usually one of our favourite land based treats. But British Rail and I weren't always friends. Next week Colin and I and bicycles boarded a train to Penge East to go to my half-brother's wedding. I was to go back to London early for yet another appointment on the same day. As we had arrived late at the station we paid our return fare at the other end and the guard wrote both our tickets out on the same piece of paper.

It was a lovely wedding and I was given an extra piece of wedding cake as compensation for having to leave early. My appointment was for 3.30. It was probably the only time in the year I would be able to get to see the chairman of Dalgety. It was always me that went to appointments like this because, being a woman and thus more used to being thwarted, I never got as upset as Colin if people said No!

In high spirits I raced to the station to catch the train back to Victoria. Colin stayed behind at the party.

'Well, I can't tear the ticket in two,' an enormous black ticket-collector grunted as I explained. 'Your husband will have to pay again – buy another ticket.' We had only just been able to afford this one.

'But we've already paid. Please write it out again separately.'

'No!' he said, and turning away started a long conversation about something else on the telephone.

It wouldn't have been important except that I knew Colin didn't have any money left for paying again. Neither had I. Just then the train itself roared in and stopped and trembled as if it wasn't staying long. It was the last train that would get me to Park Lane before 3.30. With champagne-splashed tipsy determination I started to put my bicycle on board.

'I'll leave the ticket with you,' I said cheerily and fled into the guardsvan.

'Stop!' shouted the ticket-collector. 'You can't get on that train. Get off, get off!'

He came and dragged me off and then with me fuming beside him continued his placid telephone conversation. I leapt on board again. The train's doors were all shut, the engine note changed. She was starting to move.

Immediately another large ticket-collector appeared and roughly caught hold of my skirt and pulled me off the train once more. In a flood of red Irish anger I hit him. He looked very surprised. Then he hit me hard across the bottom. We all started shouting. The first ticket-collector, leaving his telephone conversation, joined in. Heads popped out all down the train. At last the driver got out.

'Eh!' he said. 'What is all this?'

As he eventually ushered me on board, the second ticket-collector was still screaming: 'I'll have you arrested for assault! I'll have you arrested for grievous bodily harm!'

It was going to be a close thing now, I thought, to get to my appointment on time. I brushed my hair and tidied my clothes and expression. As I got out at Victoria, I noticed there were two policemen and a policewoman waiting as if expecting someone off the train. They exchanged smiles with me as I and my bicycle walked calmly past.

The chairman of Dalgety, though he couldn't have known what it had cost me to get to see him, was particularly nice and charming and though he wouldn't sponsor the boat, he sponsored our ears by saying he'd personally select and present us with some tapes of his favourite music to cheer us up while at sea.

'We want you to do a series of eight programmes for Southern Television's "Afloat" programme,' said the director. 'It will mean travelling to Holland.' He mentioned a fee. 'How would you like to become television stars?'

Colin and I looked at each other, twin gleams of hope rising to our faces. At last we had the next quarter's rent for the shed! The boat would be safe from weather at least, we thought.

Though free wine brought many a sparkle to the eyes of all the film crew on the way to Holland, food seemed almost taboo. At sea, doing six-hour watches and getting up twice each day, Colin and I had been apt to eat two breakfasts, two lunches, two suppers. Now the film unit and crew drove stoically through the eating triangle of the day while we eyed passing cafés longingly.

Finally we were at Hoorn. Thin slices of houses, with steep roofs to make up for the lack of steep hills, looked out on to the Ijsselmeer. We were on the edge of the same waterfront Edward Shooten sailed back to after he'd discovered the black monster at the bottom of the South American Peninsula and named it Cape Horn after his homeland.

We were shown on board a lovely old Dutch sailing barge, skippered by a chartered accountant turned sailor and his cheerful buxom girlfriend, our home for a week. It would probably be the last time we ever sailed across this enclosed sea, playground of so many boats, an old fisherman told us sadly. Under the water lay the seeds of the houses and farms and fields that would take its place after the plan to drain the whole area had been carried out. Perhaps the underwater land deserved to smell fresh air after all these centuries.

It seemed unbelievable to us that so many people – producer, director, editors, cameramen, soundmen, continuity assistants – should be needed to make one film. We had the easy part. We were just the words in the mouths of the cameras.

On the first day we learnt why we needed such skilled cameramen. The tripod fell into the sea and they had to hold the thousand-pound-plus equipment rock-steady on their shoulders when filming thereafter. On the second day, the skipper got very drunk and had to go out in the dinghy with the outboard to recover. In the morning he drifted in. When he saw us he yawned and stretched, and his outstretched arm knocked the unpinned outboard motor into the sea. He got his friends the Dutch Marines to go and dive for it.

Next day Colin and I had a tremendous row on the bowsprit. It was only afterwards that we realized the wool-clad microphones of the soundmen had recorded every word of it!

But it was lovely to be sailing again. Back at Southern's Itchen palace, their accountant handed us what seemed like an enormous amount of money for having a good time.

'AT LAST!' I thought joyfully, and nearly did cartwheels on his floor. 'At last we have the shed rent for the next quarter.' All was well. We rushed over to the shipyard to pay it. It took a few moments to realize that the yard manager was speaking in a tone of voice that didn't need any language.

'We've just been offered £22,000 a year for your shed,' he said. 'YOU'LL HAVE TO GET OUT BY THE WEEKEND!'

TWENTY

Peering pigs and propositioning millionaires

Getting the great hulls into the shed had been bad enough. But taking them out before their full building period was up seemed like a crime. Bill's moorings, which he had kindly offered in this emergency, were really nothing but a life-raft for the project, with a much reduced chance of survival.

Now it was goodbye to the pigeons. Goodbye to the hole, ninety feet up. Goodbye to the hopeful shavings of new wood around the hulls. The black tyre mark of the visa for the shed was cancelled. The only thing right about the occasion was the wind, which held its breath for us, and the tide, which unlike people never breaks its promises.

The whole act of taking this beautiful, delicate, half-built boat out into the open before its time was wrong. But even this wrongness we had to perform as carefully as we could.

Colin thought of using four forklift trucks, one each end, to carry the big catamaran down into the water which had been lapping eagerly around the bottom of the shed for so long. In the end, though, we decided it was worth spending our film money on the faithful Marshplant cranes which had brought her into the shed so skilfully.

We had been looking forward to rolling the muddy red carpet out for the boat's kind Admirals at a grand launching. But even this little dream had gone wrong. The eviction by the shipyard had been sudden. It had been far too short notice to arrange anything. So we will never forget the kindness of the few people who did come, and of Norman Eshley and Millicent Martin who appeared with a bottle of champagne to cheer the poor boat up and give her the luck she needed even more than if she had been gleaming and painted, rigged and ready to sail straight off as we had planned.

The catamaran slipped into the water as though she were used to it. And the tugs took over so quickly that we had hardly time to appreciate that she floated beautifully. Then we were on board and the boat was on her first voyage, to Bill O'Brien's mooring.

The size of the ropes we had to tie bowlines in brought home to us for the first time the incredibly huge size of the boat. The catamaran we had sailed around the world in seemed a toy beside it. Everything was as though seen through a giant magnifying glass. We worried and fumbled with the stiff natural-fibre ropes we had had to borrow because we hadn't been able to afford to buy proper Terylene ones. It was easy to see why handling sisal rope is a prison punishment.

Grubby pound notes were pressed into the tugmen's hands and they were off. We were alone! We were alone on board our huge floating catamaran for the first time. A gleam of pride and joy mixed with the bitterness we felt.

We looked down at our tiny Campari bobbing far down in the water at the bottom of our hulls, and wished we hadn't had to pay our solicitor by giving him our proper rubber dinghy.

Now our thick moorings looked frailer each moment. The ebbing tide roared off between its new toys, the hulls, and we thanked God and the glue-dropped bosoms of the page three girls for the sheathing. The boat seemed to be floating as light as a paper boat on the water.

We stapled some polythene over the unfinished open cabin and prayed for the long hot summer to continue. Meanwhile the first problem was, how to get off! It was such a long way down.

We staggered ashore in wet shorts, ankle-deep in mud, to be immediately ushered into the open doors of a gleaming black Rolls Royce limousine. It was the Lady Mayoress of Southampton. She'd come for the launching! But the high tide we had needed for putting the boat into the water hadn't been able to make any exception to the ruling it gave in King Canute's day. However, she bravely said she would like to be the first person to be invited for lunch on board once the boat was finished.

But the things that were going wrong weren't everything. The most valuable parts of our lives were still thriving. Eve and Jimmy were delighted that the boat was afloat. We were very proud of them. We mightn't have been very good parents at this time, but they were very good children – though they were friends more than children now. So much so that when they were offered a holiday in Wales with some friends and their three children, we felt terribly homesick. When you have no house, the family itself is the four walls, the home.

We thought again of how much more important the children were to us than a hundred boats. The boat was trying to moor us to her as firmly as she was moored to buoys. There would certainly be no room for us in our friends' car with themselves and five happy children. We longed to go. Our boat had always been our transport, but her sails were now just mirages in our minds. Our only transport was our poor bicycles. We had to get to Wales somehow. There would be many boats in our lives. But the children wouldn't be children for ever.

Determinedly we put out some extra moorings and deciding that the boat's life would need saving before ours, swopped our liferaft for a 70-lb CQR anchor, and laid that down too. Then we kissed the hulls goodbye and I oiled the rusty chain of my Wayfarer.

We pedalled off with Colin's swimming trunks bulging from the back pocket of his jeans and with sleeping bags, tiny tent and huge bags of oatmeal piggybacking on the carriers. It was just as well that oatmeal and water is sustaining even eaten raw because we kept being reminded of Pacific rower John Fairfax's attempt to cycle from

Alaska to Cape Horn. He'd had to give up because all the exercise had made him so hungry that food was costing him more than the train fare. Blackberries still grew up the steep hills as rewards, and going up hills was still like going to windward.

We only managed about ninety miles a day. But every mile was a fat mile, full of sights and sounds and experiences. Now we were cycling across the land at about the same speed as we used to sail across the oceans, though our legs weren't quite as willing as the wind had been.

Colin carried our little green tent, which looked like something you'd throw over a parked motorbike and only weighed $3\frac{1}{2}$ lb. The first night we simply dragged it over us as we fell asleep exhausted in a ditch fifteen miles on from Stonehenge.

Beautiful Wales was like a lady in need of moisturizer on her lovely face. There was no rain. Flowers in the garden smelled of Fairy Liquid and tomatoes shared the water from people's baths. I felt sad that Wales, though so needy herself, still had to provide the water supply for Birmingham. The beautiful valleys seemed all wrung out as we cycled through them.

We lost strength while cycling across the Severn Bridge and had to stop and get out our little orange plastic bowls and have a picnic of oatmeal and water half-way across. Then we cycled on with sun oil, which weighed less than clothes, covering our shoulders. We became browner than we had been ever since sailing through the tropics in *Anneliese*. In one village, a lady tourist, seeing me in my bikini on a bicycle, asked if I was an artiste from a circus troupe!

We slept among the sheep in the high mountains, we slept among the midges in the ditches. One night we were so tired that rather than do a ten-mile detour, we cycled straight through a firing range with the red flag up, cheered on by the 'baas' of the danger-money sheep nearby. Every night our sleeping bags became soaking and every lunchtime we had to spread them out and have a siesta to dry them.

We arrived in Aberystwyth just four days after we had first set off from Southampton and our trusty bicycles had not even had a puncture. We cycled into the caravan site where the children would be staying just as our friends' faithful Morris van with Eve's and Jimmy's faces grinning out of the back window arrived around the corner. The difference was, they had set off just that morning!

For the next nights we slept on a steep slope curled around each other and the stones and thistles under our tiny tent. Sleeping on the hard gaboon plywood on the boat would be a treat after we got back.

The whole holiday cost us only £5 and most of this was spent on Jimmy. I told him he could have an ice cream for every ten feet he could swim. And he kept on swimming all day and broke the bank with expensive ice cream cornets!

One of our strangest bedrooms was on the way home. On our last night before Southampton we stood with aching legs in front of a very dark opening. We were waiting with instincts straining to tell us whether it was a good place to sleep or not. In the end we found some straw nearby and went to sleep straight away. There was a rustling in the night, and strange sounds came through my dreams.

One of the excitements of my early hitch-hiking days had been going to sleep in the dark and waking up in the morning and finding where I was and what my bedroom had been like. This morning we woke up to find a circle of red-eyed individuals looking in a surprised way at us. We had gone to sleep in a field full of pigs!

We felt a bit anxious as the bikes at last bumped up the familiar potholes of Hazel Road. Would the boat forgive us for leaving her? Had the extra babysitting warps done their job?

The great boat was still there. She was floating arrogantly on the surface of the River Itchen, enormous and dwarfing the boats on all the other moorings. Indeed she seemed to have grown while we'd been away. But someone had been on board in our absence.

'My God!' gasped Colin, looking aghast at a square of white paper taped on somewhere near the stern, and the red sores of worry were opened again and I felt a pain inside that was more than my aching muscles. There was no peace.

'She's been arrested again!' confirmed Colin as he continued to stare blankly at the very unblank square on the stern. More unpaid bills, more troubles. Would they ever end?

This time the catamaran had been arrested under Admiralty Law for non-payment of bills. We couldn't move her. In fact the boat was in gaol. There were padlocks on the moorings. And next day we discovered that the only solicitor in Southampton who knew about Admiralty Law wanted £500 put down on his desk before he would do anything. We didn't have it!

All through a long summer as hot and dry as the desert and as desolate, we clung to the monster shell of the two-hulled idea which had driven us so far from the promises little *Anneliese* had made. The river police were very cheerful, but the frequent visits of their launch made a long black mark on the side of the cat and on our minds.

The seagulls were'nt as good crew as the pigeons in the shed had been. They bombarded the boat with shells as we slept and pecked holes in the thick polythene which was the open cabin's only protection against the elements.

We couldn't escape the lesson of solar energy and heat either. The temperature under the polythene at night was often three degrees below zero. And it rose to 111° in the day. The deep red Skol signs, still advertising lager to travellers on the railway curving above the muddy banks and sheds of the river, became slightly bleached in the fierce summer daylight.

The sun got us up the same time as itself each morning, when it became too hot to stay inside our polythene home. Our faithful polar sleeping bags would have made the devil himself too hot after eight a.m. each morning; though at night they were needed. For a time the boat proudly wore its only piece of cabin equipment, a large smart brass barometer and thermometer donated by a kind supporter. Then one day the mercury, driven mad by its daily frantic career upwards, burst its tube.

We'd worried about being separated from the children for our holiday. But now we had to lend them to our friends during term time, so that they wouldn't suffer and so that they could be clean enough to go to school. We cycled the four miles to Hamble and back each day to see them. The money from the article we'd done on our cycling marathon to Wales came in at last and paid our friends something for their board. It seemed a very hard time.

It hadn't rained yet since the boat had been out in the open. When it did, what would happen? Colin wondered. The scorched wood and peeling paint gave no answer.

But the clouds beyond the horizon must have been listening. The day that we began painting a plastic protective coat on the boat there was a downpour. The virgin dryness of the long hot summer was over. The Sikhs' prayer had been answered. The two-month-old dust, as well as the graffiti, was finally washed off the cars parked in Southampton streets.

But neither clouds, nor sun, nor the nights' darkness could hide the fact as we had hidden ourselves on the boat, that time was drawing on. What were we going to do?

There was no doubt the whole project was flat on its back. Before it could get anywhere at least it had to stand up and walk. I felt we were letting everyone down from Bing Crosby to *Anneliese* herself. From Eve and Jimmy to the editor of *Penthouse*. It was miserable.

Colin went on painting the boat during dry intervals and I painted my silver shoes again.

'You can have a modelling fee,' said the editor of *Reveille* after I'd scrubbed a few of the shipyard layers of dirt off. 'We'll take twelve portraits of you for the competition. Then the readers will arrange them in order of which they like best. The winner gets a car.' He then admitted that this weekly competition usually used puppies or kittens as subjects. 'But,' he added, seeing my face, 'we do sometimes use girls too.'

So I was staggering on down the fund-raising trail again, though the first part would all be wasted on solicitor's fees. All my journalistic training told me that the story of the boat had already gone on too long. There had already been several beginnings, several middles and several endings . . . though none happy. The old silver shoes were on their seventh tin of spray paint. The same plots were unfolding over and over again.

I cheered up when Jim Fox, the gold medal winner, Roy Castle, Harold and Mary Wilson and Ted Heath all joined our Admirals' organization. But their subscriptions were just Special K rations.

A few real hopes flickered when it seemed possible that an aluminium company was going to give the boat a mast. But in the end they said they couldn't see the sense of putting a large gesture towards a boat still called *Skol International*. It really seemed she couldn't have that name and further serious sponsorship from other sources.

But we still wanted to repay Skol for their earlier kindness too. Would they mind sharing the name with another company? we asked one day. They reacted as though we had dealt them another shock.

'No,' they said eventually. 'Rather than that we'll give you back the name altogether.'

It was sponsoring monogamy. It was a very sad moment. Really it felt like a divorce. Allied Breweries and the boat had been separated for some time, but we had always hoped that there would be some way in which they and she could be reconciled. Now it was really all over. The end of the relationship, the end of a dream. The money they left in was just alimony. The boat was back to her maiden nothing name, and apart from still being under arrest, a free woman again.

Our ploys were getting wilder. The line between obsession and madness was getting thinner. Scholl gave me a pair of clogs. I sprayed them gold and threw my old silver shoes into the dustbin. It gave me more confidence. Suddenly I thought back to the *QE2*. Our very first sponsorship money for the boat had come from Japan – hadn't it? Why not try again there now?

So I took advantage of the kindness of our insurance firm and borrowed their telex machine to send several telexes off to the Far East. The only reply came back: 'Our chairman Mr Hittot has been dead for three years – but his soul wishes you well.'

The following week we were invited to a dinner by the Swiss Ambassador, and I told him about this. 'Never mind Japan – why don't you go to Switzerland? You were born there after all,' he said. I told him we'd already tried. 'Ah,' he said, 'but this time I will give you a letter of introduction and you shall see the President himself.'

I filed this at the back of my mind. We certainly couldn't afford to fly to Switzerland just now.

We arranged to meet the chairman of Wills for tea at the Savoy. The theme tune that cigarette people had sponsorship money to spare played over in our minds.

I had met this chairman once before. He was a charming, attractive man whose love for his little house in Ireland where fun could run riot was as great as his love for tobacco. But I wasn't sure if I could recognize him again out of the context of his office.

We sat awhile in the foyer near the main door of the Savoy and first recognized Mick Jagger who passed by having a row with someone who looked like a business manager. Then a large, cheerful chairman-type man walked in and smiled at me. I rushed up and kissed him on the cheek.

'John Wilson!' I said enthusiastically.

'Er,' said the 'chairman', helping himself to a second kiss, 'Er – I wish I *were* John Wilson ...'

'*Rosie!*' cried a cheery voice a few minutes later. This time it *was* John Wilson. There was really no mistaking him. But a watchdog of the Wills' purse walked a few steps behind. And as our discussion went on I began to realize that once more, a pleasant afternoon was probably the only result of our meeting.

Time went on, we were swimming harder, barely keeping level in the ruthless tide. The new year brought with it the present of a new bicycle. But the five-speed Puch was to make up in heartache what it saved us in leg-ache.

'Er – excuse me, Miss!' A policeman moved after me as I cycled away from the traffic lights near Earls Court. 'Is that your bicycle?'

Maybe he wasn't used to seeing someone in a fur coat and golden shoes riding a five-speed yellow racing bicycle. 'That's a man's bicycle isn't it?'

I smiled and pointed to the little red child's seat on the crossbar. I praised him then for caring about stolen bicycles and said if he ever saw anyone *else* riding this bike to be sure to stop them.

Two weeks later it *was* stolen. The thieves had cut through the three chains we had used to shackle it to the railings. They had only bothered with the racing bike. Our faithful wallflower Raleigh, not knowing whether to look pleased or hurt, still remained. The thieves had hung the three cut chains mockingly across the rusty crossbar before they had left. We never got it back. To forget our grief we plunged again into the seething morass of the latest Earls Court Boat Show.

Something about people's attitudes to our boat still puzzled us. When oil wells became paddling pools, the type of boat we were trying to develop might even, with its superior speed and unsinkability, bring back the commercial days of sailing again. She would use, without surtax, the huge income of the world's wind, instead of the dwindling capital of its fossil fuels and the rogue elephant of nuclear energy. Why then had we found it so very hard to get the sort of backing she needed?

Now, as we had another brush with the conventional sailing world, we suddenly had a revelation. Surely it couldn't be that people were prejudiced against catamarans, could it?

Had we really aimed so high that the arrow had fallen

behind us? Had it been a mistake to try and build something new, a prototype boat for a traditional yacht race? We'd certainly made a fine mess of the whole project.

If we didn't get enough sponsorship by Colin's birthday on 4th February, we decided gloomily, we'd have to give up. Our poor boat, far from being finished, was still actually under marshall arrest for unpaid bills. But the battle was still on: 4th February was still a long month away.

In a brave moment I kidnapped the surprised chairman of the Nat West Bank Group away from a stag party at the Boat Show – and tried to persuade him to write off our overdraft!

After this vain attempt I began to think seriously of what the Ambassador had said about Switzerland. But I really couldn't let the President down by hitch-hiking to see him.

'You've got nice long legs,' said the swimwear department of a glossy London store providentially. 'Come and do some modelling for us.'

A week later the fee had been turned into fare. I had arranged to fly to Paris and take a train on from there. I left feeling I was gasping under the excess baggage of heavy responsibility again. But Colin didn't dare leave the boat. Anyway, he said, since he was ten years older than I was, I ought to have extra trouble and worry so that I could catch up!

I was standing at Charles de Gaulle Airport, worrying and feeling a hundred already, when a dark-haired man with a shrewd look in his brown eyes came up to me and said:

'You've probably never been on a boat. But there's something special about you. Would you like a job as crew on one of my sailing yachts?'

TWENTY-ONE

I could have been a film star

'Instead of my becoming crew on one of your boats – why don't you become an Admiral of our boat?' I answered, half-joking.

Then I showed him a picture of the huge catamaran. His eyes lit up as if he was looking at the pin-up picture of a beautiful woman. Firmly he took hold of the photograph by one hand and me by the other and led us off to a nearby coffee table. It was ridiculous. The person I was meant to be enthusing to about our boat was the President of Switzerland! There was something a little bit unreal about this present situation.

'I would like to do more than just become an Admiral,' my dark-eyed wizard man was saying. 'I would like to sponsor your yacht entirely.'

There was something about the way he spoke. I couldn't stop a strange surge of excitement in my body. I felt sure he was going to be involved in our destiny in some way. It was the Pendle magic again.

It was most likely that he was just a businessman looking for a companion for the night in Paris. But something in his manner suggested otherwise. After all, I had first met Colin at an underground station – why shouldn't I meet our sponsor at an airport? I was twenty-seven now. I'd already had more years to study the nature of predatory man than most Oxford dons have to get their PhDs and flowing robes.

'Your boat is the fastest-looking sailing boat I have ever seen. Faster than all my ninety other yachts in Greece,' he went on. 'By happy coincidence my name is Victor. She will be called *Victor* too – for victory around the world!'

He said he owned the largest fleet of charter yachts in Greece.

'You will be surprised how fast I can make things happen,' he told me enthusiastically. 'Tomorrow you will fly with me to Düsseldorf Boat Show and then we will go to Greece and arrange it all!'

The letter to the Swiss President was heavy in my briefcase.

'But actually,' I told him, hesitating, 'I'm just on my way to Switzerland, to see the President about the boat ...'

'But there's no sea there,' he exclaimed.

Next day over lunch his eyes glowed brighter and browner as he described how *Victor* could sail around the world faster than any boat had ever done and then as queen among his fleet come back and do a tour of honour in Greece, and he would be king of charter fleets in the Aegean and Mediterranean.

After lunch he rang up Bill O'Brien and had a long conversation with him.

'Bill is the kind of man I like to do business with,' he said afterwards. 'He speaks the same language as I do even though we come from different countries. When he's finished with your boat he must design other boats for my fleet.'

Our horizon, grim and grey for so long, now looked extremely beautiful, and it wasn't just the wine that made me happy. Victor was a mystery man, come out of an aeroplane from nowhere. I felt I could trust him, but could I trust my own judgement? If only I had some advice. If only Colin was here, I thought.

It was nearly Colin's birthday now: the time we said we'd give the whole project up if we hadn't found help. But the contents of the letter to the President of Switzerland burned in my head. And somehow, I knew I had to go there first.

'OK,' said Victor. 'But don't be a victim. There are too many victims in the world.'

Two days later the train and my heart stopped at the

border. Stomping uniformed figures that might have been ghosts from thirty years ago seized my papers and went away. We were somewhere in the no-man's land between France and Switzerland.

What was wrong? Two babies in the next compartment started crying. An hour later the officials came back.

'Your passport,' they said with a pair of frowns. 'It was inaccurate according to the records!'

They had actually changed the birthdate. Those officials had just stolen three of the years I thought I had lived away. It was very strange. Once more I felt my life wasn't real. I felt much older instead of younger as I arrived at Berne, near my birthplace, at five minutes to midnight. A courteous Swiss grabbed my bags from the station platform and deposited them and me on the steps of the nearest hotel.

'Herr Furgler will see you on Monday,' Dr Hug, his personal aide, said early next day. He said it as if I had won the pools. But it was a blow. My purse didn't really allow for one extra night in a Swiss hotel, never mind two, even if the manager did follow the charming Swiss custom of putting red apples on the bedside table.

The whole weekend lay between me and the President. I knew no one in Berne now. But I wasn't alone. Perhaps I was nearing the edge of madness after all. Perhaps the strain was beginning to show. For a spirit from my old hitch-hiking days was with me and was soon luring me off to explore. Go to famous Gstaad, it said, and see the stars over and under the snow mountains ... It would pass the weekend away and I could go for almost nothing.

Haystalks prickled my face above the drawstrings of the sleeping bag. The haybarn where I slept the next night was as much buried in snow as I was in hay. The light-years of seafaring, marriage, writing and children slipped away. It was like the old days when I used to go hitch-hiking in Lapland.

However, bright eyes that reminded me of our friends in the London bedsitter peered out from the gloom of the shed. They seemed to wonder why I did not share their hayseed as they had often shared human crumbs. At six o'clock the sound of the first car of the morning acted as an alarm clock call. The driver of the second became my anonymous chauffeur to Gstaad itself.

'GSTAAD MY LOVE' – said the posters in English. The roofs of the secret chalets on the hillside, like the boughs of the dark green trees, seemed to touch the snow. They contrasted with the neon boutiques in the main street. I went into one shop to try and get some gloves.

The manageress held out a newspaper. What was printed I couldn't understand. But our photographs were unmistakable. Colin and I and Eve and Jimmy smiled out from a crisp page. What a pity, I thought, that the picture couldn't change into flesh and blood. Jimmy would have had such fun throwing snowballs here!

The manageress frowned at my woollen dress with the hayseed around the hem, and at my Dr Scholl clogs. She carefully got out a gold lamé skisuit and boots which together only cost three times the return air fare to Switzerland.

'Wear these while you're here,' she said smiling. 'I will lend them to you. You were born in Switzerland – you are Swiss. It is only right!'

At Gstaad railway station stood an antique Rolls-Royce. The driver bowed at my enchanted gold lamé suit and pointed up to a hill about two miles away on the top of which, complete with turrets and towers, stood what looked like a palace from a fairy story.

'Palace Hotel,' he said and ushered me into the Rolls.

The manager welcomed me kindly as I introduced myself. It was a long time to midnight but I really felt like Cinderella now.

'Stay here tonight as our guest,' he said, trying to decipher the drawing I'd done in the glossy French copy of *Enfants du Cap Horn* which I'd just presented to him.

The snow turrets of the mountains were even more beautiful than the turrets of the Palace Hotel. A determined cable chair, dangling on a wire that seemed too thin, pulled me up and up that afternoon. I hovered over the fast snow where skis sped, over the topmost fringe of the lovely dark trees and into a cloud so thick I was glad I wasn't navigating. Then I was out in pure sunlight on pure snow under a bright blue sky. I had arrived at a white summer near the top of Switzerland! The top of the world.

Two hours later I was just stretching my legs out in front of a lovely fire in the Palace drawing-room when a very small, interesting-looking man with brown hair and intense eyes came and sat down beside me.

'Good afternoon,' he said politely. 'The manager lent me your book. It is wonderful! I think it would make a very good film. I think,' he added studying my red face so closely it made me feel uncomfortable, 'I think you could act in it too ...'

'Oh no,' I thought, shuddering and thinking of the pornographic film our one-time business manager had once suggested. I diplomatically changed the subject to skiing and his face lit up in a different direction. Twenty minutes and a cup of tea later a porter came with a message for him and he got up and left. I left too and went up to turn on the gold taps of the bath in my suite.

'Who was that gentleman you lent my book to?' I asked the manager later.

'Roman Polanski,' he said. 'He left for Los Angeles half an hour ago!'

As I slid into the silk sheets I couldn't believe that only last night I had been sleeping in a haybarn with the mice. And the silk sheets now felt even softer because my skin had been made sensitive by the haystalks of a night ago. As I left the manager pressed a gold keyring into my hand – 'A mascot!' he explained.

The Swiss President welcomed me courteously with a pot of coffee. Switzerland may be a democracy, but here as elsewhere in the world, I found that the higher up people were, the more kindly and polite their manner. Even in England, I had gone to see chairmen because they were generally the least frightening people in any company and the most like my own family. Now a male secretary and aide sat down at the polished wooden table and neatly took down every word we said.

I told the President that although Switzerland had no sea, I thought her people had the courage, caution and determination of the best sailors and that I was very proud of having been born here. The clerk's neat scribbling must have oiled my tongue, for I carried on telling him that if it hadn't been for the chance of my grandmother having a fancy for a little girl with curly blonde hair and adopting me when I was three, I might still be living in Davos, speaking nothing but Schweizerdeutsch! Learning to ski instead of to sail.

The President said that our boat couldn't fly the Swiss flag unless I gave up my English passport. But that this difficulty could be overcome if she was sponsored by a Swiss firm, and that meanwhile I must come home and play softball with his family. I hoped that by now the last of the clinging hayseeds had gone from my dress.

The following afternoon a charming reporter and photographer from the chief Berne newspaper took my photograph beside the famous Berne bearpit which I had last visited in frilly four-year-old's dresses just after I had been adopted. I really had no more idea of what was going to happen now than I had then!

The batteries in the chink of light at the end of our tunnel faded rapidly over the next few days, as I tottered down the long mental tube feeling my way, visiting Swiss firms, realizing that the President's golden key of introduction which he'd handed me didn't fit any of those independent Swiss companies' coffers as easily as he had liked to think.

Victor's brown eyes seemed to haunt me. Perhaps he had put a spell on the companies I now visited.

But it was a thrill to meet the actual chairman of Ciba-Geigy whose harder-than-wood glue, including the aerolight and resorcinal types which had been used on both *Anneliese* and the new monster, were famous throughout the world. It was the glue Colin had sent a taxi all the way up to the north of England for! This chairman had the talent of stretching a few of his valuable minutes to make it seem he had all the time in the world for you.

'No,' he said sadly, pouring out some coffee for me, 'it really isn't our policy to sponsor boats. My friend Herr Furgler made a mistake. But I would be privileged to sponsor your boat in a small way personally.'

Another special person I met in Basle was the ex-King of Sweden who gave me part of his soul when he gave me his sextant to sail around the world with me.

Colin's birthday came because no barricade of failure could keep it away. I sat desolately in Berne Yacht Club entertaining the only dog who ever joined the supporters' club. Admiral Nelson was a giant St Bernard who made his signature with his paw! We had passed the date we'd agreed on to bail out from the project. Now we knew we'd never bail out. We'd land our large sailing aeroplane somehow.

Back in the shipyard we sank kneedeep in mud and worry that should have been sand. I thought more and more about Victor. His promises were now like fresh rain to someone dying of thirst. He was an oasis in the middle of our anxieties. But his numbers were always either engaged or didn't answer. He didn't answer his telexes either. Perhaps the oasis was just a mirage.

At last I caught his secretary's voice on the telephone. New York, Istanbul, Chicago, France – Victor had been to all these places since I'd last met him. He seemed to orbit round the world like a sputnik. He was now in Munich. He'd be there for five days. She mentioned something about one of his planes which could take me from Paris to Munich.

None of my adventures abroad was anything to what Colin was undergoing at home. The boat was still under arrest. He really couldn't leave it.

I'd have to go alone again and find Victor. It seemed

that my caution had lost more than it had gained. The weeks to find sponsorship had run out, the boat was in danger of suffocating from lack of the oxygen of time. If we left it too late, all the magnificent meals of money in the world couldn't help her.

I packed my bags. Out of rebellion at having to go away again so soon the zips wouldn't shut.

TWENTY-TWO

'I am the King of Bavaria – get in.'

But Victor's aeroplane wasn't waiting at Paris Airport as arranged. My last few francs slipped casually across the kiosque de téléphone counter. For once I got straight through to Victor's Munich office.

'My plane crashlanded near Cologne yesterday,' he said, sounding below zero depressed. 'But it'll be quite easy for you to travel to Munich by train instead. I will be here for another three days.'

My half-sister Anneliese after whom our first boat had been named had been killed in an aircrash. Fate had been kindlier this time.

'Come by train!' The way he said it, it sounded such a sensible and easy alternative. There was just one problem. I was travelling to Munich for the purpose of fixing up a multi-thousand-pound deal for the boat. I couldn't really let him know I didn't have the train fare to start with! I had been relying much too much on that aeroplane.

A friendly taxi driver gave me a lift to the start of the autobahn to Germany. It seemed a long long way. I was carrying a light bag, but a heavy weight of responsibility. I was no carefree hitch-hiker. Truly I must be going about this assignment foolishly. But for the moment there seemed no other way!

I moved away from the French male hitch-hiker who sidled up to me on the verge, whispering 'Voulez vous compagnie?' He was dressed in a greasy black leather jacket and smelled strongly of stale sweat. It was back to *Rosie Darling* days.

My first lift was with a man who kept adjusting his trousers. But at least he took me almost to the main autobahn to Germany. At last he stopped in a stubble field and wanted for a fifty-mile drive what my naked chairman had offered £10,000 for.

But I was able to open the door and run faster than him. I felt a bit frightened and sickened and too old for all this nonsense. But I had to go on.

Twice I stopped, climbed into the autobahn-side ditches away from the zooming traffic and took out the little orange plastic plate which was one of the ones Colin and I had used on our oatmeal picnic on the Severn Bridge last summer. Now I hungrily ate some oatmeal from the small packet I'd bought before leaving Paris. Same Severn Bridge meal, but oh so far away.

Each lift was an uneventful hundred miles or so onward towards Victor. The radios provided most of the conversation ...

Strasbourg hadn't changed much since the time I'd last slept under one of the picturesque bridges. Then I had slept well curled up like a shapeless brown lump in my sleeping bag, chameleon-coloured with the bridge itself. I had no sleeping bag now. To be truly homeless is to have no sleeping bag.

By midnight I felt the temperature must have risen, for all the cold was now inside my body, ravishing me more thoroughly than any man could. Morning came at last and the growing light showed a bird, possibly a thrush, on the pavement near me. The poor little thing was dead, frozen stiff. I buried him in some leaves.

The full stomachs of the early morning workers began to pass me by. A man at a newspaper kiosk winked at me. A lottery person came up and asked me for some coins. She wouldn't have, if she had known where I'd slept.

A large shiny foreign-looking car was approaching. It had a strange numberplate. I did my special: 'You have been chosen to give me a lift' sign. But it swooped by. A few minutes later it reappeared on the opposite side of the road and turned round and stopped by me.

'I am the King of Bavaria,' the driver said regally. 'Tell me where you want to go.' It seemed like something out of a fantasy. But I climbed in. By the shadows of the following day we arrived in Munich.

Victor's office was huge and the walls shimmered on an indoor horizon. Large maps lined the walls and there was a picture of Victor himself with a yachting cap on. The yachting cap was slightly askew as he came in half an hour later.

'I'm just off to buy a footballer for the Greek National team,' he said. 'Come with me. We can discuss the boat afterwards.'

Young men with football muscles under blue jeans crowded into the famous Munich Football Club restaurant after practising in the floodlit stadium outside. Victor bought a husky young footballer and his parents, arranged for them all to go to Greece and arranged for himself to fly to England to meet Colin and Bill O'Brien. It was all done in alternate conversations of German and English over one plate of steak and chips.

He still seemed very enthusiastic about the boat. But now there were a lot of other things on his mind too. He told me that I would probably need a third more sponsorship than I asked for, which was a refreshing change. But added:

'You should have come with me before. I had more time then. You were determined to go to Switzerland. It was a pity. Now I have an even more important project than your boat for you to handle. I wish you to sail one of my yachts to Abu Dhabi and sell some of my beautiful land to the rich Arabs. It will only take a month or two and your commission will be over £200,000. Then you can sponsor your own boat.'

£200,000? Arabs? Could I believe him? But it was two months' sail out there from Greece. Our next goal, the Round the World Race, started on 27th August, and a crowd of days had passed since the deadline of 4th February. Even £200,000 in three months would be too late.

There always seemed to be someone listening in when I spoke to Colin on the phone. I felt a desperate need to go back to see him and the solicitors. So as soon as I had

Victor's letter saying he'd sponsor the boat and for how much, I hitched home with it hot in my pocket.

Victor said goodbye cheerfully, but I thought the light in his eyes had died a little when I'd said no to his project.

Waiting, waiting, waiting ...

I had met a fairytale sponsor, someone we had always dreamed of. And I'd let him go off before anything was properly signed and settled. I left the final arrangements to international telephone wires more tangled than any kitten's ball of wool. It seemed to me I had written yet another chapter in the handbook of How Not To Get A Sponsor!

Wednesday five p.m. GMT came and went; and next week came and went again. Time itself had broken the sound barrier.

'He's coming to England to see you,' his secretary said. 'He's in California now, but just for a day or so!'

The catamaran looked exasperated with us. The square of plywood we put over the arrest notice was getting old and blackened. To cheer the boat up I went to see yet another London chairman. He invited me to lunch. But his expression encouraged me to wrap up the bread from the sideplates for tomorrow's breakfast.

The loud screech of brakes as I stepped outside sounded like my own heart stopping. Suddenly an old woman was lying in the gutter moaning. I dialled 999 from a nearby phone and then ran out and covered her up with my coat to keep her warm till the ambulance arrived. As it drove off ten minutes later I realized that my carrier bag which passed for a handbag was lighter. My purse had contained five precious pounds. They had gone.

Three youths were lolloping away down Charing Cross Road. One looked back towards me. It must be them, I thought grimly and set off. I kicked off my golden Scholl clogs and thanking 'lovebirds' for my fitness, ran after them as fast as I could.

In the early morning you have to avoid tripping over

sleepy dachshunds in the park. Now it was people and they are much bigger. By the time I caught up with the youths I was in a completely different part of London. I must have run for two miles. They were puffing more than I. The jacket of the biggest youth tore as I caught hold of it.

'I expect you only took my purse for fun,' I gasped hastily, seeing his big fists. 'Can I have it back now please?'

The blond one with the face redder than a shepherd's warning sunrise kept staring at the pavement. I felt a bit scared. The policemen were all too busy arresting motor-cars to be around now.

'Aww give it back,' said another. 'She's had the guts to run after us ain't she?' The other hesitated, then burrowed deep into a denim pocket.

'It was only a lark, Miss,' he said smiling sheepishly. 'We've been to the pub.' It was wonderful to have the notes back. It was more than just the money. I felt I had at last succeeded in something.

Then I looked down at my feet. They were bare. I was near Marble Arch. The well-dressed dummies in the shop windows pouted. Even they had shoes and they didn't need them. Where *were* my shoes? All at once I realized that they were two miles away.

I ran back through the bristling elbows of the lunch-time crowd. A dustman had pulled up in Cambridge Circus. A man was sweeping the pavement. He picked up a pair of worn golden clogs from the gutter, and lifted them high. The mouth of the dustbin opened expectantly.

'STOP! STOP!' I yelled. 'They're mine!' The man handed them over with a pitying glance.

TWENTY-THREE

Crumbs of hope

The next journey my golden clogs made was to Guernsey. I felt a real responsibility towards the long deserted pockets of Colin's suits from more prosperous times, because that was where my ferry fare had come from. I was being driven mad waiting for Victor to contact us. I felt what had gone wrong was all my fault. I had to do something.

'Try Fort George,' someone said as I arrived on the island. 'There are lots of wealthy people living there.'

Somewhere on the thin line between obsession and madness I persuaded myself that I only had to knock on someone's door and they would give me money to finish the boat. These houses were watchdogs of Guernsey residents, which guarded fortunes of millions of pounds. One large pink house looked friendly and it had a lovely garden which cheered me up.

An imposing lady with a smile sparkling as brightly as the jewels round her generous neck answered. But her smile of welcome faded when she saw it wasn't who she'd been expecting. 'What do you want?' she asked suspiciously. I saw the grim set of the face under the mask and shuddered.

'Er ... Er – I was just passing and I wanted to tell you how very beautiful I think your flowers are.' Then I smiled tremblingly and fled.

The icy wind straight from France wasn't as icy as the feeling inside me. I cursed myself for a coward. By the time I had walked up and down the road outside Fort George's gates half a dozen more times, it was almost dark. The wind howled. Soft warm lights came on in many windows.

I felt an alien from outer space. I had to try one more time.

'Are you a Jehovah's Witness?' an old gentleman asked in a quavering long-distance voice.

'Don't be silly, Albert,' said a compact-looking lady coming up behind. 'She's the sailing girl.'

I stammered and tried to explain why I had come. I felt less comfortable than I had in front of audiences of thousands during book promotions.

'Well!' the woman said eventually. 'Here's a pound. I'll give you another when you go round Cape Horn again.' There had to be a better way.

If a friend in a strange place is someone you've met before, I rang up my only friend in Guernsey. With his kindly expression and brown sea-going face, Roger Fuller looked even fitter than he had when we'd first met him nearly two years ago.

Maybe it was because he went ocean racing every weekend. Maybe it was because he ate his own delicious Granary bread. It had sprouted wheat grains in it which Christopher Columbus would have given his captain's cap for.

We had been to see oil companies and sheiks. But we didn't use fuel. We had been to see cigarette manufacturers. But I didn't smoke. We had been to see frozen food manufacturers. But we never had a freezer on board our boats. We'd even been actually sponsored by a lager company when I was no lager drinker.

I knew that Roger's business interests included health food companies including Granary, ship chandlers' shops, and shipyards. He was not only a person whom we would like whatever he did – he was one of the few chairmen we'd seen whose product we really thought great. Unfortunately I knew he already owned several ocean racers and was unlikely to want to sponsor our monster.

He took me out for a delicious salad. For pudding he arranged that I should do promotion for Granary to the value roughly of what we needed so desperately for the next insurance premium.

I decided to ask his advice. Next day sitting in his office

at his home, sipping a medicinal glass of brandy and wearing very un-nautical red tights from Berne, I told him about Victor.

'It sounds a sensible arrangement,' he said looking at Victor's letter. 'You can use my telex machine to try and get in touch with him again.' He read the letter again and an idea seemed to cross his kindly face.

'If nothing comes of it,' he added, 'and you can't get another sponsor in time, I'll try to do something. It would be a pity for the boat not to be finished in time for the Round the World Race. There isn't much time, is there?'

I still felt that if Roger Fuller did sponsor the boat, he would be doing it mostly out of the kindness of his heart, because he wanted to see an interesting boat finished – rather than because he really wanted to be a sponsor.

I had just finished putting a spoonful of black molasses in his coffee as requested, when the telephone rang. It was Colin on the telephone, saying 'Nationwide' were going to give our boat 100 minutes over a period of time and that they would be coming over to our Jersey lecture.

But the chink of light at the end of the tunnel kept appearing, then being blacked out again. Hope, when there was any, seemed just a mirage. At last Colin arrived in Jersey. Both he and his seaboots looked worn out, and his eyes had a mad look in them.

'I probably won't be able to come to your lecture at the St Helier Yacht Club tonight,' Roger said sadly. It was just as well. Perhaps all the strain and stress has been too much, I thought. Colin had completely changed. He was rude and talked too loudly. He was on such a different wave-length from me that our conversation capsized. 'Trust me, trust me,' was all he would say.

But my stomach felt all screwed up with anxiety. It was worse because we went to a rival yacht club before the lecture and were deluged in double brandies by the friendly members. Mixed with the cocktail of the sleepless nights Colin had had they had an evil effect. I too felt dizzy from the brandies and from skating so near the edge of failure for so long.

Anneliese looked the same, as the film we usually showed ran through the course of our voyage. But there the similarity with any other lectures we'd done ended. The prosperous members with well-lined lives and insides still sat in rows as the lights went up. But their eyes were staring in a way they'd probably not stared for twenty years.

Colin was standing on the table in his seaboots. 'You are not a good audience.' He held up a large white card on which he had crayoned the word 'APPLAUSE' then another one 'LOUDER' and 'QUIETER' and 'LAUGHTER'.

I couldn't believe it. I sat shaking. This, not the hard wood, was the real toll of all our troubles. I wished the wax the doctor had syringed from my ears was back so I wouldn't have to hear this.

He was shouting louder now. '*I want you to get out your chequebooks*,' he was saying, '*and write cheques for £150,000 for the boat*.'

The audience sat as if stunned. I felt so sorry for Colin. I'd always thought things were tougher for him than me. Women seem to live on the edge of failure for so much of the time. But a man has a more sensitive skin against the knife of disappointment. Then he rushed out into the night.

They were all looking at me. Somehow I stood up and gave my prepared lecture. The nice ones listened and asked friendly questions afterwards. They understood Colin had been under a lot of stress. The pompous ones, the ones more accustomed to spending the weekends sailing through gin and tonics instead of seawater, weren't too sympathetic. They never forgave us for the staring look we'd brought to their eyes. But it was all an accident as much as falling in the sea is.

Afterwards I was rescued by a charming tomato farmer and we spent all night driving from wild coast to wild coast of the island of Jersey searching for Colin. I was sick with worry. In despair I went back to *Red Lancer* and went to sleep. At four a.m. two policemen woke me up. 'Your husband has admitted himself to hospital,' they said.

I rescued him and his stripy pyjamas they'd given him, first thing in the morning. We went back to Roger's boat, to the smell of the sea to recover. We'd already paid a price for the boat that wasn't money; that was irreplaceable. Now, I thought determinedly, everything must go right. I didn't want to burden Roger with it. So we went to see two of Colin's contacts – and stopped envying millionaires.

The first one was a lonely, unattractive man who couldn't even get anyone to crew on his motor yacht with him. The second, a billionaire arms dealer, had art treasures on the walls of his mansion and wars on his conscience. Though quite pleasant and charming, he looked rather fat and unfit. They were both interested. But it takes time for the plant of sponsorship and business to grow from a seed. There wasn't any more spare time now than spare water in the Sahara.

Someone wanted either me or Oliver Reed to open a school swimming pool by diving into it. But the water had been turned off for a week, so there wasn't time for that either.

Visiting those other millionaires made us very proud of Roger. He was so splendid and fit and looked as if he enjoyed life even though he was rich. We always had wanted only very splendid people connected with our boat anyway. Now natural selection seemed to be making it so. But would he really do it?

Roger had told us that it wouldn't be necessary for us to come up to Granary's board meeting at Burton upon Trent next week. So of course, we had to come. We zipped up the little Force 10 tent which we'd been living in, and which had long ago been blessed by the witches of Pendle Hill, shook the bits of grass and four-leafed clovers off our clothes and caught a long train north. There were only three months left now to the race itself.

The large gloomy old mills around Granary Developments had been turned into splendid nurseries for Granary bread. Each one of the many floors in each building showed a different stage. Pure dry wheat, the same as survived thousands of years in the Pharaohs' tombs, was from time to time poured down in giant funnels from the top storey into great tubs on the floor below where it was soaked for two days.

Granary crew, wearing white wellingtons kept specially for the purpose, then spread the damp wheat out on the acres of floor, where it was allowed to sprout for a few days before being turned over. If it wasn't turned over, they told us, the wheat would continue to grow almost to the low mill ceiling. So the secret process would go on. Finally the grains would emerge still whole in the famous Granary bread.

After our tour we were made at home in a comfortable office, while a meeting roared on in the boardroom next door. We could hear Roger's pleasant voice from time to time above the others. Someone came in and collected the sheaf of figures we had prepared. They seemed to be talking about the catamaran at last. '£20,000,' we heard someone say and the voices answered with the usual negative note. But our figures added up to more than three times that, however low we tried to make them.

We waited and waited. We both knew this must be almost our last chance for the race, and our last strength to get sponsorship for the boat was on overdraft from happier times already. The batteries of the gleaming idea which had already driven us into and over so many difficulties were fading.

At last Granary Developments' genial financial manager came out.

'Would you like to step into the boardroom, please,' he said.

'Can we get it sailing for only £20,000?' we asked Bill O'Brien on the phone half an hour later. 'Ah yes,' he said soothingly. 'Sure you can.' But he didn't tell us how!

Now the shadow of the giant Skol factory in Burton upon Trent fell across our pleasure at being involved with a new sponsor. Were we making the same mistake all over again? Had we learnt nothing? The past was a bad teacher. We were just as tempted to accept too little as before.

The boat herself remained out on the river, tugging at her sisal warps; the target of the beaks and bums of all the local seabirds. Worst of all, she was still under arrest.

The days fled by. We couldn't get any of Roger's £20,000 till we had paid the £2,000 to have the boat unarrested. This was the first half of the amount that the boat builder was suing us for. But we didn't have it. Meanwhile the free winches offered so kindly by Lewmar were slowly being withdrawn as it seemed less certain we'd be ready in time for the Round the World Race. Speed seemed more important than any rights and wrongs of a legal hassle now.

Someone once flatteringly said that the sound of me frenziedly crumpling up my rejected pages of writing was like the sound of pound notes being screwed up. I told Colin this as a joke: a gleam came into his eyes and he made for the nearest public telephone and dialled 01 for London.

Selling an unborn book seemed a bit like getting your child a job three weeks after he's been conceived, and I felt really nervous when I went to London for the appointment Colin had arranged with the publisher. But the editor was so kindly that I confessed the real reason I needed a book contract.

Three million words on the telephone later, he'd arranged for a cheque to be counter-signed by a director of their branch a hundred miles away and brought by special courier to London. Somewhere in the sandwich of my meetings with the publisher I had a tremendous row with my agent who said I shouldn't negotiate books myself and anyway it wasn't enough and if his other clients like Agatha Christie and Paul Gallico behaved like me, they'd still be on the dole. It was so bad afterwards I no longer had an agent.

But I did have a cheque which would save the boat. It

was a lovely cheque. I felt like stroking it.

The advance on my next book should have been to live off, but just now, at this lovely moment, the boat's life seemed the more important. I leaped into a taxi and just got to my solicitor's office as he was closing his coat buttons and the door. He stared at the cheque, then opened his mouth slightly: 'It's no good! It's made out to you, it ought to be made out to the plaintiff's solicitor.'

Neither commuters' rugby elbows nor traffic jams could stop me as I fled back to the publishers again.

The all-important Granary board meeting to confirm their sponsorship was tomorrow. The boat had to be unarrested by then. And for the moment the price of my book and my agent had left me just as badly off.

'Please,' I gasped, bursting into the editor's office just as he was leaving. He listened as benignly as if this sort of thing happened to him all the time.

'Tomorrow,' he said, 'I'll have it redone. It will be at our country office at nine o'clock tomorrow.'

By the time I'd spent the night with friends and gone to the country office and re-collected the precious cheque, it was ten the following morning. The cheque lounged lonely in my wallet. All my money had gone. A spitfire pilot, a salesman, a racing driver and a garbage contractor were my anonymous chauffeurs as I rushed back to Southampton with my mouth thirsty for a 10p cup of tea but with a cheque for £2,000 frisking in my purse.

At one minute to the twelve o'clock meeting I burst like a tattered Cinderella into the office. An undipped beam spread across the solicitor's cherubic face. I handed the cheque over trying not to think of all the work I now had to do to earn it. Within minutes he was on the telephone to the Admiralty Marshal. For the moment the boat builder was satisfied. Within minutes the boat was free for the first time for over a year. The only chains holding her now, I thought, were the trusty anchor chains.

At the twelve o'clock meeting, Granary were able to give the go-ahead for their £20,000. Next day, to celebrate, Colin and I went to lunch with *The Sunday Mirror*. They got us roaring drunk on tomato juice and brandy and we signed a powerful contract with them. Of course it wouldn't give us any money now. We never seemed to earn any money till we were at sea. Then we didn't need it.

We decided to spend the night at a friend's house to recover. I fell asleep in the tube on the way there. Colin had to prop me up and at the same time pretend he was just a Samaritan and that he didn't know me. I just wasn't used to all this high living and drinking.

On arrival I excused myself, went up to the bathroom and fell asleep again! I woke up in the bath with our friends' five-year-old daughter sitting beside me, patting my hands and singing to me.

My Granny always used to say that troubles, like deaths, come in threes.

The boat had been built through a Guernsey company which we owned and which had been formed specially for building the boat. It was ironic, because usually only people with millions of pounds have companies in the Channel Islands. We were only rich in the kindness and trust of the hundreds of ordinary people like ourselves, like the lady with the £1 and the little dog, like Police Sergeant Commer of Wimbledon, who'd put their faith in us and the boat.

But now, just as the boat had been unarrested, new sponsorship found, trouble struck again. Our company fees hadn't been paid for a long time, now the States of Guernsey threatened to dissolve it and seize the catamaran. And worst of all, our accountant, who had been patient for so long, now refused even to speak to us.

Then the Nat West Bank threatened to foreclose its loan on us and grab the boat too. I had already given the lifeblood of my next book. There was no publisher to save us now. Colin ranted and raved and went mad. Jimmy cut his own hair with the scissors. Eve alone upheld family honour by getting fifty out of fifty in her spelling tests week after week.

The race, the race, the race haunted us. It was the boat's débutante coming out ball, we couldn't bear her to miss it.

Meanwhile, as troubles with the boat raged on, we still had to earn enough personal money to eat. There were no social security hay bales for us children of the sea.

The financial situation was temporarily eased when Colin and I went to London to be photographed as *Woman's Own*'s 'bionic couple'. Colin got £300 for having his hair cut and we spent all afternoon leaping over the high class dog turds in Hanover Square. Since the light was bad, they seemed to expect us to do it in slow motion too.

But it didn't last for long. Colin said he felt like a kettle with the lid on but boiling inside. The kettle had now boiled dry. Everything was in turmoil.

Because the children were going to school in Hamble we had moved our witches' Force 10 tent to a nearby campsite and shared our sleeping bags between that and the boat. BBC 'Nationwide' who meant to film us on the race came down to our tent and after being chased about by our campsite commandant who seemed to think they were spies, they did a film of us mixing our millet and water for breakfast and counting out our last twelvepence in the world to give the milkman.

My friend the witch said you always get what you ask for in the way you are prepared to receive it, not always in the way you expect.

'I'll buy you a monohull for the Round the World Race,' said Roger. 'Give up the catamaran.'

The Committee told us we wouldn't have to do trials in a monohull, it would be ready-built. It would not be just a monohull, it would be months of time he would be handing back and we could fulfil our contracts – could we? Did our Admirals, did the little lady with the curly dog care about the race – or our beautiful catamaran? What was the right thing to do? The poor catamaran was still caught in a spider's web of legal green string.

But fate, never asleep in our lives, stepped in again. With a monohull our lives would be organized like a shining robot. But without a heart. And fate cared. She stepped in with both the monohulls Roger tried to buy.

'Let's paint the *Rosie's Granary* name on now!' shouted the BBC producer enthusiastically. There she was, the first of Roger's beautiful monohulls, with long black hull and gleaming winches. She did look a splendid boat, though special in a different way from the catamaran.

The paint brush had nearly touched the hull when the agent for the boat came rushing down the jetty tripping over the cameras, goggling around at what looked like a Goldwyn-Mayer film set.

'Can I have a word in private with you?' he gasped. 'You mustn't film it. She's not meant to be in this country. She's not for sale after all.' It was all off. On whose side were our spirits now, I wondered?

The next monohull candidate was more certain. The film crew had filmed Roger signing a cheque for the deposit. And I'd presented Roger with a celebration bottle of whisky which someone had given me in London the year before. Then suddenly the owner, for no reason other than the prodding of destiny changed his mind and said no.

'We'll keep in touch,' said the BBC producer as we turned dejectedly out of Lime Grove a week later. A man playing an out-of-tune mouth organ in the subway had ten pence from each of us. It seemed likely we should be in the same profession soon.

I was reminded how the previous week Colin had given another ten pence to an old gentleman near London Road, in Southampton. Immediately a crowd of other hopefuls had gathered.

'No, no – go away,' Colin's new friend had said to them. 'Leave him alone – that's *my* gentleman.'

We retreated into a Wimpy Bar to think. Perhaps we could go as crew on another Round the World Race entrant and at least manage to do our filming for the

BBC. But it seemed unlikely.

'Another catamaran!' exclaimed Colin, suddenly looking up from his third cup of coffee. 'We'd still have time to do the trials in a catamaran that was finished already.' Perhaps our poor monster wouldn't be so unhappy if we went in another of her own breed, I thought sadly.

'No!' said Bill O'Brien when we rang him up, and the power of his voice made us hitch-hike all the way back to Southampton to find out why.

Early next morning he drove us off in his yellow car. The first stop was a café where he treated us to coffee and fat jam doughnuts. There were bits of the blarney stone in the jam in those doughnuts.

'I believe you *can* finish the 70-footer for the race,' he said in the quiet tone of voice that before now had changed the whole of our lives. We had sailed around Cape Horn in one of his catamarans when everyone had said it was impossible. Now sitting in the café with our feet firmly on the ground everything seemed possible.

Perhaps the reasoning of the blarney stone was that we wanted to believe him too. I felt enormous relief at the thought of not deserting our big boat which already meant so much and which had been through so many experiences with us so far, even though helpless and half-built.

'I will help you by doing any additional design work and by giving any technical advice free,' and his words were Irish gold.

A few days later an article came out in the *Portsmouth News* saying that our 70-foot catamaran had already sailed 30,000 miles, which surprised us. But they did say some true things too. They said that great projects needed great men behind them, and that it was not really round the world sailors who needed the most bravery, but sponsors.

Finally Roger's strong broom had swept away our cobweb of troubles. Or so we hoped anyway.

'I know another RAF man like myself, to whom I can

communicate my instructions easily. He will finish your boat in time,' Bill said. So we went to see Fibreglass Bill, a modestly termed king of boat construction, and his dog, his partner.

Each morning I did my high kicks on the beautiful decks of *Rosie's Granary* and began to feel again the power of the spell binding us together. We were making love together and the climax would come when she was finished. It was a personal thing, not really to do with race committees, sponsors, the telly and the newspapers.

Oh to get her finished, to get her finished, I thought; to pull in the main sheet and let the wind fill the mainsail for the first time ...

But it was time to stop dreaming. Dreams are popular because you can do them even while you are asleep. Reality is harder. We got our first Granary money and paid a mechanical Brontosaurus to clear a site for the boat in Willment's Shipyard.

The next day a tug purred up to the big cat. Ten minutes later she was being drawn swiftly down the river, leaving practically no wake. Her light hulls made less impression than a Stone Age plough in the water. We borrowed tyres from a seething proprietor based on the other side of the yard and Colin and I, clad in our wet-suits, slid them under her delicate hulls as she grounded. This time there was no tyre 'visa' stamped on her side. Her arrival was just marked in the mud underneath.

They started sanding off the paint so that the deck could be sheathed with resin before it rained again. The cataraman sat proudly enjoying the attention. Another of her twice-nine-squared lives had started.

'Don't think,' said Fibreglass Bill. 'If you think of the alternatives now, you can't do it!'

'We might have to be a week late starting. We might have to be towed across the startline. But we will make it.' The voice in my head was clear. But did it echo against Bill O'Brien's blarney stone?

So we let the clovers grow up around our little tent in Hamble and moved permanently back to the eternal mud of Willment's Shipyard.

'I sees it all in me 'ead,' said the gallant chippie as he got out his knife and to our alarm started to cut away the tattered polythene which was all the cabin top had been for so long. The magic had started again. 'I sees it all in me 'ead,' repeated the chippie and began to build one we would bump ours on.

The stern was blocked up carefully till it was high enough to sit on specially-made giant trestles. Protective resin sheathing began to spread over the huge deck. A sea of brand new wood shavings sought their freedom in the mud below. The boat looked so pleased with herself. The noise of the electric drill was like music after a century of silence.

The first night back on board we slept under the sky.

The second night, new wooden frames arched over us.

The third night, we had a home with a roof.

Our feet were through our jeans at the sound of the first footsteps on the ladder each morning. By the time the building team clambered on board, the sleeping bag would be rolled away in honour of the resin drops and we'd be brewing coffee. The first to arrive always was black belt karate expert shipwright Graham, whom we'd last met repairing the ravages that always seemed to be befalling our cabin on the *QE2*. All that seemed a long long time ago now.

Early the following week I took the King of Sweden's sextant to Kelvin Hughes in London to be checked. I was gazing longingly at the beautiful chronometers in the reception room, when a smiling man came up to me with a small package.

'I've been waiting for you for three years!' he said, handing it over. He looked like a wizard. It was the little deckwatch which had been all the way to Australia and back round Cape Horn with us. It had survived the gales but had got lost at the mender's and we'd been heartbroken. Now there it was again. Looking all pristine and new, keeping the secret of all the storms it had gone through inside its shiny face.

'I've rated it for you,' the smiling wizard man said. 'It's working perfectly.' It would make a fine consort for the King of Sweden's sextant.

Now a hundred things competed fiercely for every moment of the day. The materials and the building team worked feverishly to keep up with each other. Five hundred damp charts had to be dug out from deep in the hulls, and weighted down with the as-yet unfitted mooring cleats, as I sorted them out on deck. Coral islands ... Rio ... South Africa ... a thousand memories jammed my mind. We were still stuck deep in the mud in Willment's Shipyard, but I had the whole world on deck with me. A young Israeli who had just sailed through the Southern Ocean himself came and helped with the laminating.

'Will you be off again soon?' Colin asked him.

'Oh no,' he replied. 'I've just come back. You need five years between long voyages. One mustn't be greedy.'

It was nearly time for us to go. We watched Bill's human partner sculpture the first of the huge rudders out of wood and filler and knew that our five years ashore must be nearly up.

If we were really going on the race, we must think about crew. People might be harder to bear than storms at sea. But we should have to get used to this. The boat didn't need any crew other than us, but the race did. For the moment though, the only definite crew member was the fine 500-watt Racal Radio they'd kindly lent us. It was the big sister of the one we'd had on board *Anneliese*.

'They'll think you are a ship when they hear you,' Racal's chairman Ernie Harrison said after he'd generously offered to lend it to the boat. I was glad that the radio examiner in Sydney had taken such a shine to Eve and Jimmy that he'd given their parents 70 per cent each in the third class radio operator's exam.

The agonizing over how high the cabin should be and whether the wind or the humans should be humoured and made comfortable could have gone on for weeks. But there didn't seem a second to spare and before the first week of building was out, our cheery mercurial chippie had constructed a cabin with minimum windage and which only Eve and Jimmy could stand up in.

We solved the problem of which shape the cabin windows should be by having no windows at all. The bullet-proof perspex Bill had obtained for the moment lay sulking on deck. Two hatches which had been bought as escape hatches for the floor, but were too small, were put in the roof instead, giving the boat two round eyes for us to see through.

Next week the shipwrights offered up the starboard rudder and the first excited white licks of undercoat were going on in the cabin making it look a bit like an igloo. The weather did its work too, by keeping fine. Even our fingers had to uncross so that we could help with the work. At last the project itself seemed set fair.

High grade oil of enthusiasm oiled all the tools. Everyone crammed fifty hours of neatly stowed work into each day. The huge boat obsessed and delighted us all. Someone lent us a caravan on site and Eve and Jimmy were delighted and helped by entertaining Fibreglass Bill's dog as he worked. It seemed as unthinkable that we should ever have given up this boat as it seems to a hungry person that he has ever been full and fat.

Each day began with taking Eve and Jimmy to school in Hamble by train, taking advantage of British Rail's free 'seats' for bikes – and then cycling the four miles back with our daily two loaves of Granary squashed on the carrier behind. It was satisfying as the days passed to see the rash of Granary wrappers spreading through the local shops as we spread news of the *Rosie's Granary* boat. We really wanted to be worth our keep to Roger and do the best we could to repay him for his courageous kindness to us and the catamaran.

Jimmy even took two loaves to his Harvest Thanksgiving. They were an offering more real to us than any flowers we could have sent. They were put in the centre of the altar, and delighted Jimmy gazed at them hungrily all through the service. God must have liked them, for next week we were presented with 4,000 yards of best quality webbing for our trampoline.

We felt the quality of our lives was improving. The fight is almost over now, I thought gratefully.

TWENTY-FOUR

How I became a nun

'Don't run after a bus or a woman or a man,' the old saying goes. 'There's always another.' People have been hurt by running after all three. So why did the next race on the horizon always seem the only one? Why are false gods so large that they fill the horizon?

The paper napkins of the expense account lunches our insurance company had so kindly treated us to in the old days had now given way to grim paper forms to fill in. And a stream of bewildered surveyors began to visit the boat. The remark of the first was echoed by the others. It was: 'I can't survey this boat, because I have never seen a boat like it.'

It was the first shoots of a new crop of troubles on a fertile soil. However beautiful the boat, however graceful, however strong, we knew that Granary couldn't afford to let her sail a yard unless she was insured and she wouldn't be insured in this case unless she was surveyed.

The senior stressman from Plessey's came and pronounced her the strongest boat to enter the race. Bill O'Brien, more confident than our own nerves, suggested a ten-foot drop test. He then did an unintentional drop test of a weight on his foot and Fibreglass Bill had to get his instructions by the designer's bedside.

In the midst of all this the real storm broke. The blarney of the doughnuts was still in our stomachs as we ran out of time and money in a photo finish. Roger had always wanted the very best and most expensive equipment for the boat with his heart. But his pocket and our budget from his company didn't agree. The compromise had been too expensive.

Also the fact that the bills had been paid by a company belonging to a millionaire had made equipment manufacturers unlikely to proffer the cheap deals and easy terms they might have offered us. But really it was our fault. We were writers, photographers, sailors. But a clerk typist at our solicitor's office had more business training. We'd shaken hands with Granary over the ghost of Skol and once again had sold the name too cheaply.

We knew the thunderbolt from Granary was coming, but it still stunned us.

'You've overrun the budget,' they said. 'No more finance till we can have a board meeting in ten days.' In fifteen days the race would have started.

The first day of Southampton Boat Show came faithfully round again. There were the same hills, same faces, same white tents slightly more weathered.

The air had long since been saturated with millions of words of planning about the rig, the mast, the sails and general layout of the big catamaran whose fate was still so uncertain. I thought back to all our marathon meetings with the grey cells of the sailing world and felt sad.

To cheer myself up I admired some oilskins which had buoyancy and a safety harness built into them and found I had just volunteered to perform as oilskin test pilot and be thrown into the water at 20 knots and then towed from the harness through the icy water at high speed by the Inshore Rescue. Luckily I somehow managed to borrow a wetsuit off a stand to wear underneath and so was far warmer in the water than I had been when going round the Boat Show looking at equipment.

I'd just struggled salty-skinned back into my clothes when a man in an immaculate chauffeur's uniform came up and almost saluted.

'Sir Eric — saw your interview,' he said, his voice polite and clipped as a tame hedge. 'Would it be too much trouble for you to come with me now? He would like to help you.'

The shiny fittings at the Show reflected my failure to be able to pay for them. Five minutes later I was climbing into a Rolls Corniche for a ride of a hundred yards to a nearby hotel. Half an hour later and the story was still growing. I was sitting in a hotel suite at a long glossy table that carried the weight of the words that must have been spoken over it in many a boardroom. Then a tall distinguished man, with a little grey hair sneaking around the corners of his head, came in. He clasped a golden cane as if he owned the world, which perhaps he did.

He laid the cane at my feet then went to the sideboard. Something went click, click, click as he moved. I wondered what it was. The champagne he handed me was the finest I had ever tasted and two glasses later I had to concentrate to think why I was in his suite.

My eyes kept falling on the lovely Harrods' box in the centre of the table. Pearl strings, the fringe end of a mink coat and pieces of tissue paper poked out of the corners. The man had the scent of richness upon him. But he didn't look happy. He still clicked whenever he moved. But now it seemed quite a pleasant sound.

'We must get down to business,' I thought, 'before the champagne makes us too fuzzy.'

'Er ... your chauffeur said you might be kind enough to do something for the boat.'

He looked at me and his eyes seemed to outgrow his monocle. 'You never need to worry about finance again Rosie darling,' he said. 'You can have anything you like ... IF ...'

He bent over towards the Harrods' box. His hands shook a bit as he undid the golden clasps at the side and lifted the lid. I gasped. It was like a strange treasure chest inside: gold, diamonds, fine blond hair pieces, three mink coats heaped up inside like so much garbage for the collector.

He drew out two long black candles in golden holders, lit them and sent the twentieth-century light back into its wire. Then he burrowed beneath the mink and jewels and reverently lifted out a pile of plain cotton clothing.

It was a nun's habit!

'Put it on,' he said.

'OH NO!' I thought. But it looked so pure. It was only the simple fancy of an old man.

'You can put it on in the bathroom,' he said, pointing to a door at the end of what had seemed to me a boardroom to start with, but had changed so much since. Oh well ... *click, click, click* the man went as he opened the door.

Ten minutes later I looked in the bathroom mirror and saw a nun's face. I really looked innocent and pure. Surely this was harmless. If the man was religious why should I mind? The silver cross he'd given me to wear as well chilled my neck. 'He's a bit daft – but what's the harm,' I thought again.

I felt peaceful and calm and thought of the Holy Sisters in Ireland and the one Jimmy had spied reading an Alistair Maclean behind her Book of Prayer. Then I opened the door ...

... and there was this naked man with a metal leg. He had a can of three-in-one oil in one hand and he was oiling it. The light from the black candles glimmered. The silk stockings he'd also given me to put on underneath my habit stroked my legs now. I had thought it strange, for a nun's dress is too simple for these.

The faces of my children, my husband and my grannies and the boat all flashed through my mind as he walked stiffly towards me with arms outstretched. There must be another way, I thought once more ... If it depended on this, the boat would have to go!

I rushed back to the bathroom, grabbed my clothes and fled. It was only when I noticed that people were standing aside for me and being politer than usual that I realized I had reached the streets still dressed as a nun.

I felt sad as I walked along. Why was it people had such strange needs? Was it just rich men who had these fancies? Or did the poor just have no time?

A week later we were standing very desolately by the dock of HMS *Vernon* in Portsmouth. Not only had we missed the race. We had even missed its start because we couldn't afford a taxi and our rusty bicycles with the children's seats in front had been too slow. Now all the boats had gone and with them, not all, but enough of our dream to have inspired us for the past two years. There was a vacuum of hope that the grey lapping harbour water could not fill. It was pouring with rain and the puddles sloshed around inside my leaky yachting shoes and I felt below-zero miserable.

Well, at least I'm not standing here in a nun's habit, I thought. But what were the real ethics? If I had been a whore, the boat would have been sailing a year ago; the children would have had the best of everything; Colin would have had a naval blazer with brass buttons on it. Was my private body more valuable than all these?

When I got back I found Fibreglass Bill had left a lovely bouquet of flowers for me in the caravan and a poem which brought tears to my eyes. But if things were as bad as they seemed we'd surely have to keep too cheerful for tears. Tears are only safe for those secure enough to be able to be blinded by them.

The boat now seemed alive, seemed to talk to me each morning telling me to go on trying. Not to give up. We had no money. But words at least cost nothing. We had another meeting in the caravan.

Owen Parker – Edward Heath's skipper – arrived as a new sorcerer on the scene. Proctors the mastmakers, Spencers the riggers, David Mackworth of the rolling furling gear makers, and Fibreglass Bill were all there. It was almost like the old days, except that we missed Austin Farrar and the benign and clever influence of John Powell. The same play was on again. But with a different cast. We had always wanted two rollers for the foresails, so that we could reef easily. Now we discussed having one which would swing from side to side. The boom staysail with the easy reefing points was rejected.

Bill O'Brien wanted a 60-foot mast. Roger said that would look too low, and what about the boat's performance in light airs? Bill said that the boat could go better in all conditions with a low mast. The extra height would be wasted weight. It would just twist and cause tipping couple. He really recommended a three-quarter rig.

Colin, in a moment of enthusiasm, felt that just because the mast was shorter and the biggest sail smaller, we needn't lose extra area by the smallest sail being even smaller as well. He suggested that the staysail go to the masthead. If the jibs went down each side of the boat, they would give lift which you needed in all but very light airs, when you actually needed the bows down for a sharp cutting edge through the water.

There seemed a dizzying number of alternatives. One thing was certain. The boat could only have one rig at a time. And until she went out sailing, no one could quite know what was right. A boat like this had never been built before. A boat like this had never been rigged before.

A boat like this would never ever be finished, unless Roger managed to persuade his board to put in more finance. We were gaily discussing the best mast, when the boat had no prospect of any mast at all. How had so much enthusiasm grown out of the desolation of the previous week?

Roger and his decision flew off to Mustique to start some new chandler's shops in the West Indies. We and the boat stayed at home and waited ... Then he cabled: 'NO MORE FINANCE UNTIL WE KNOW IT CAN BE INSURED.'

During Southampton Boat Show we had actually managed to lure a Lloyd's underwriter from his niche. He had crept gingerly about on board the catamaran. He looked as though he felt that catamarans were boats from another planet. Finally he said: 'I would like a surveyor friend of mine to do a full survey.'

Mr Winterbottom arrived fresh from the Nile, where he'd been surveying a boat which was going to be used in the filming of an Agatha Christie thriller. It turned out he'd designed Tom Lack's Catalac catamaran and unlike some of the others he didn't seem to think the boat was a spaceship from another planet. But he stepped cautiously on board anyway. He ordered an extra building menu including more frames in the hulls and then said that subject to his approval Lloyd's would insure the boat.

It was a big moment. We forgot that for the moment we hadn't the extra finance to do the extra building anyway. Time kept being gobbled into the past. The race, even part of it, slowly faded from our horizons and compass headings. We thought it ironic that one of the few unsponsored yachts should have arrived first in Cape Town, on handicap.

Two days later the producer of BBC South West's 'Zodiac' programme bumped his way through the potholes of Hazel Road to make a film of us and the mud and the new Granary sign which had just been lovingly painted on by the same signwriter who had done *Anneliese*'s name in gold leaf so long ago.

He had to take my fingerprints for the benefit of the programme's palmist, who would be appearing in the studio with me. Our fingerprints had already been taken once when we'd opened Barnes Police Station. Now as my thumbs were rolled in the black, I felt as nonchalant as any other second offender. The weather was fine, but the BBC sound equipment gave up. Colin managed to save the situation with his own tape recorder, but lost the remains of the last of our *Woman's Own* money out of a rebel pocket when cycling to collect the children. It was an expensive film for us!

Two weeks later we crawled by coach to do the 'Zodiac' programme with John Cleese. You had to hide behind screens, nodding into a monitor if you agreed with what they said – and how could you help it, it was all so complimentary! But one thing caught in the sieve of my mind. 'You will go on many voyages,' the astrologer said. 'You will get into terrible scrapes but always get out of them again. There is a silver thread running through your life, reach out your hand, touch it whenever you need to and it will help you.'

It had been quite hard to get clean enough to go on television again. I wore the same brown crochet dress from Tahiti which I'd wriggled stickily into as we'd sailed past the Eddystone Lighthouse on our way back to Plymouth. What spoilt it was that I had a terrible row with Colin just before I went on and to make up I said all sorts of nice things about him on the air that I didn't mean and he didn't appreciate as he sat scowling just behind the cameras.

At last another cable arrived from Roger in Mustique: 'FULL GO AHEAD ON CAT' it said, 'IF BILL O'BRIEN WILL OK 70 FT. MAST.'

'No!' said Bill, 'I'd still advise a 60-foot.'

During the next few days the metal would have got hot without any furnace if it had known how its length was being argued over. And the mast was just the first of the decisions which now had to be made.

One possibility was a 65-foot mast boom staysail, centre-handed light large genoa.

Advantages: Bill's magical lift; controllability; tipping couple and control of light genoa in very light airs so that the bows would be down; no tipping couple in other conditions; very flat sheeting possible. It would also look like the original painting that had inspired us.

Disadvantages: it was expensive and nobody knew for certain that it would work.

The other possibility at this time was a 65-foot mast centre strut to the front beam, cutter rig, possibly a centre roller.

Advantages: it was more conventional; Roger might be more pleased; it would be handier for short tacking, and likely to sail moderately well anyway; it was the sail-maker's rig. Most important, it was less expensive. The boat was now like a beggar collecting pennies from Granary, never quite sure when the next might come.

'You don't look much like your picture in the magazine.' One of the normally respectful yardmen came up leering in a way that alarmed me.

'Oh no!' I thought. 'Not *Penthouse* again.' But the boat-builder from next door was proffering a thumbed copy of *Woman's Own*. There we were, billed as 'Britain's Bionic Couple'. Colin was in a gleaming white tracksuit, I in white shorts and top, all of which had been snatched back hastily after the photographic session! The rubbish tip above the shipyard where the final full page colour photograph had been taken looked like an African safari park.

Next week a film unit took a fascinating ten minutes of me writing my third book. The typewriter was glad because although the books had travelled the world even more than our boat had, the typewriter who had done all the work had only ever been seen by my grimy fingers.

TWENTY-FIVE

Eve and Jimmy – honorary bulldog puppies

Next day the building team climbed back on board *Rosie's Granary* again. Drills whirred, wood flew like confetti and the coffee kettle sang. The theme tune of progress was playing again.

I treated my hair to a cheap conditioner. It turned it bright red instead. This must have had an effect on the inside of my head as well. Or perhaps the red rust had been brushed to the outside. For I bought six 15p jotters and blew the dust off the Dutch-faced Remington which had been a kind present from the chairman of that company.

A book about our voyage of experience over the past two years was bursting to come out. It was no good pretending it didn't matter. It had to be written. I was thrust into the schizophrenia of a writer living two lives at once. While I was climbing on board the 70-footer I was also climbing up the slippery steps when we had first arrived back at Plymouth after our round the world voyage. I was back to the days when Jimmy peed on the green carpet in the Holiday Inn because he thought it was grass. How things had changed since then!

Our only pet on board *Anneliese* had been a cockroach called Cuthbert. What sort of animal could we afford to have as a friend now we were so poor?

'15p each!' said the rather dragon-like science teacher, handing over two little black mice born and educated in the local comprehensive school. We popped them into a specially prepared empty peanut butter barrel, then strapped it on to the bicycle carrier and the little mice were off on their first ride. A little later they were selecting themselves a new home from the pet shop – by climbing in through the bars!

The smallest one christened my finger and herself Nipper. Her larger sister accepted my old black mare's name – Columbine. She had the same glossy black coat and kindly nature. It took man centuries to discover how the wheel worked. But the two little mice learnt all about theirs in roughly half an hour. They also discovered toilet roll tunnels and that tissue paper is pink wholemeal food for mice.

We didn't have any television in the caravan. But the mice were much more entertaining than anything you might need a licence for and we sat up late till red rings circled our eyes and watched them for hours. Columbine might be BBC1 we decided, Nipper BBC2.

Like our friends the birds in the Galapagos, the mice seemed to like things that were moving and changing. If they moved away it was not out of alarm, but because nothing had changed and they had got bored. Every moment not dedicated to fun was wasted in their opinion.

That night we thought we heard a squeak coming from the caravan cupboard and wondered if it was a boyfriend already coming to court the two beautiful teenage brunettes. They kept us awake all night and we kept them awake all day. Their bright black eyes gazed at our bleary ones. It was a happy confederation of insomniacs.

Perhaps they knew that we had once shared a London bedsit with more than fifty mice, because they quickly became our friends. Soon they started helping me write my book. They had great sport pulling pieces of typing paper across the table. And sometimes people coming into the caravan would be startled to see two little glossy black animals with large gleaming eyes peering out from my hair, or sitting on my shoulders washing their faces, though not mine, with tiny delicate pink feet. Sometimes they performed daring Cresta runs up and down my arms. Sometimes they disappeared among the keys of my typewriter and I had to watch carefully that they didn't get a sudden headache.

When we had got to Cape Horn I had felt a sense of wonder. Others had sailed by hurriedly in a veil of wild spray but we had stopped and had an illicit meeting with the wild black rock. I'd had a feeling that we were privileged, that this was a place human beings weren't supposed to be. I now felt the same sense of magical privilege looking at the little mice sitting happily in the crêche of my cupped hands. As I watched Columbine climb cheekily up Colin's trouser leg, I couldn't help thinking how alarmed the girl had been in the King Kong film. We must seem like King Kongs to them.

Soon Eve's early Christmas present was walking all over us, waggling her fat behind, pausing now and then to pop something else into the bank vaults in her mouth. Demelza the hamster seemed really surprised that Eve didn't keep such large stores of food in her bed as she did in her posh cage. Certainly when we cleaned out her bed with its rotting food supplies, she seemed as alarmed as a businessman would be if his savings were taken away.

Erich Fromm said that there are two sorts of people. The havers, who get their security in life from having things, lead anxious lives because possessions can always be taken away and when you die you can't take them with you anyway and so worry about dying. The other people are the 'Be-ers', who take joy out of each moment of each day, just out of the magic of being. When they die, they've had so much fun and interest that they laugh with their last breath. The mice kept reminding us of the be-ers and we tried to be more like them and not worry too much.

In spite of all our difficulties we had thousands more things to be happy about than we had had this time the previous year. At least the boat had a cabin now and was no longer out in the river at the mercy of marshals and seagulls. At least the children were living with us and the four fragile walls of the family still stood secure. And the book was getting fatter as well as the mice. The dark clouds gathering above the boat were real ones now and gave the deceitful impression of themselves giving shelter.

'Progress will only be delayed by the weather,' Fibreglass Bill prophesied.

To our astonishment we discovered that scaffolding cost only about £8 per foot to hire. Soon it was growing up from the mud each day. At the end of ten days, an amazing metal forest with sheet tin leaves had appeared over the boat. *Rosie's Granary* crouched beneath it gratefully. The butterfly had gone into chrysalis. Colin and I climbed all over our new roof and stopped even the tiny nail holes with filler and masking tape.

Mud still squelched in through the holes in our shoes and came out at the ankles. Most of our food went to Eve and Jimmy with the crusts for the mice and it really was quite hard for us to get enough money for food. But then Colin and I had once fasted for five days as an experiment without harm. At least the dream was crawling ahead on its pennies. At least the beautiful cat under the cold tin roof was sitting proudly in the dry, and the music of hammers rang out each day.

Language is a lick over the surface of communication. People see the shadows of the shadows of reflections of what goes on in other people's heads. Lice jump from head to head more easily than thoughts. Colin and I had been through so much together. But did we really know each other? If he knew some of the things I thought about I knew he would go mad. We lived in one little caravan where everything, every sniff was shared and seen. I valued the last stronghold of the privacy of my mind. One of our favourite hobbies had always been talking to each other. But we were two sharp flints rubbing together, and as the sparks flew we only scratched the surface of understanding.

Anyway, now the boat's difficulties faded to manageable size compared to really important problems such as what to do about the mice's wheel which kept going wrong. And how to keep Demelza from hibernation. One day Colin and I decided once more to resist the temptation of dried soup and watery gruel and go on another fast.

The caravan was orbiting round and round. We were sitting there helplessly, light-bellied and -headed and totally spaced out, when there was a knock on the caravan door and a Princess appeared. She smiled the smile of somebody I had known well all my life without meeting. Her hair was as black as Cape Horn and her eyes immortal.

'Felcign Gervais and Keith.' She introduced her equerries.

'If ever you feel you would like a change and a warm log fire to sit beside – we have one!' Keith said kindly. Felcign Gervais just climbed on to the caravan sofa, and put one champion paw protectively against Princess Tracey's shoulder.

We still didn't quite believe they were real as we called round to see them at their Woolston address later that evening after cycling the children home from school.

But Tracey herself opened the door. And there, silky and solid, was the first bulldog any of us had ever seen. Twopeople or Stonesteps Saffron sat with a proprietorial paw on the arm of her own special armchair. Her black, black eyes twinkled and gleamed with good-natured wickedness and fun. I couldn't stop looking at them. They were human. But more than that, they were just like Tracey's eyes.

Twopeople jumped off and welcomed us with her whole body. My heart thumped in a way it never had when meeting any famous person. Twopeople was more than a dog or a person: she was magic. There was something really special about her. Bulldogs, we heard, only live for about ten years, but those eyes looked centuries old.

Now she climbed back on her armchair and sat there laughing with her lover Felcign Gervais the boxer at her feet. Pictures of boxers, painted by Tracey and hung all round the walls, seemed alive in the firelight too and kept the other two company.

In a corner of the kitchen was a family which made all the multiple births at Hammersmith seem as nothing. They belonged to Mantru Diamond Lil, who had had a record litter of thirteen bulldog puppies on 13th September, our wedding anniversary. It was so strange. Fate was taking a hand, laughing around us somewhere.

Now the puppies were just becoming 'people' and they looked up at us with bright eyes and soft pink noses with tiny black spots on; their sturdy little paws with a long way to go in life now tore up the pictures of the Page Three girls who lined the floor of their pen.

Twopeople, who was eight months old, had the same exuberance as the little puppies. It seems that bulldogs, like our little friends the mice, never grow up and never die. They live in eternity through their joy of being. Tracey said that Twopeople got her nickname because she was brought up with some basset hound pups and was never quite sure whether she was a bulldog or a basset. Now she looked at me with those eyes and I felt she was putting a spell on my life.

Wanderers like us don't really miss not having a house, or many possessions, or even the pleasure of seeing a tree grow year by year. But now I watched the children play with the puppies and an ache which I'd had inside me for years suddenly ceased. I felt my heartstrings being played by a purer love than you can ever feel for humans. It was like the love I'd had for the animals who were my only friends as a child.

Now it was happening again. I was falling in love in a way the boat forbade. Tracey understood. She handed me a piece of paper. On it carefully written out was Kipling's poem:

> There is sorrow enough in the natural way
> From men and women to fill our day
> But when we are certain of sorrow in store
> Why do we always arrange for more?
> Brothers, sisters I bid you beware
> Of giving your heart to a dog to tear!

Eve and Jimmy got white hairs on their clothes and became honorary bulldogs too!

We were just the lug worms who lived down Hazel Road. We'd never known anyone in Woolston really well.

We exchanged advice, money, autographs and smiles with the people who came to visit us. But when they looked, they looked not at us but at the air around us. The people we loved were usually thousands of miles of ocean, earth, trees and roots away.

Now at last here were people close by who actually seemed to care about us. Keith and Tracey came each day with treats for us and our hamster and mice. Our bicycles became used to leaning against their garden wall in the evenings and their stove became hot with delicious meals Tracey cooked. Tracey's paintings were beautiful. But she had got one hundred per cent for cooking in her school-leaving exams as well as one hundred per cent for art. Her chips could be made into lollipops and the meals fed the eyes before the stomach by looking beautiful.

Just two weeks before Christmas there was another boat crisis. We'd overrun budget again. The boat would just cost what it would cost. We couldn't help it. But of course we still stood in our leaky shoes and felt guilty about it. The chrysalis was shaking on the branch again.

We had struggled to save our giant so many times in the past two years. This time there loomed the sharp dark rock of the next instalment on the legal claim to the boat-builders that the book advance had chopped the first part off. It was a rock which should have been navigated round by our *Mirror* earnings on the race.

'Roger may try and sell your boat, his board may force him to.' Sad hints flew back and forth through the cracks in our fingers over our cupped ears. All the tools stopped working and devoted themselves to their hobby of rusting again. The boat herself now stood desolate once more, deserted and cold under the tin sheets of her shed. It was quiet as death.

Just as we felt we were at the very end of our tethers, that our dream would die, something lovely happened.

We were stumbling along in the quicksand. The voices of the children asking about a Christmas we couldn't afford were a pain in my ears I could hardly bear, as their Christmas stockings were shrinking in the hot wash of poverty. Then Keith and Tracey and their bulldogs came and kidnapped us back to their Woolston oasis for Christmas.

Instead of palm trees, there were toys, mountains of sweets and chocolate. There was a rubber tree instead of a Christmas tree; and instead of ordinary Christmas puddings, our insides smiled round special Harrods ones. There was an enormous turkey, the king of turkeys, and stockings for Eve and Jimmy bulging more than the fattest lady's and heaps of roast potatoes cooked with the spell of Tracey's special secret recipe. You can eat plain bread in rich company and be a millionairess in happy feelings. But we had all these treats as well and I knew that this lovely Christmas would be treasured in our minds during the dark wild watches and struggles ahead.

Keith took us up to a spare room and went over to where a beautiful three-storey cabinet with a glass front was standing. He hesitated for a moment and seemed to swallow vigorously. Then he asked 'Would the mice like to borrow it while they are here?'

Half an hour later Columbine and Nipper had their own ladder linking three levels, and a lace crochet curtain. The ground floor was their bedsit, the middle floor the gymnasium with the wheel, and the upper storey was the bar and also the nature playground where the branches grew toilet-roll tunnels.

It was only afterwards that we learnt it was the £90 cabinet Keith and Tracey had been meaning to fit in their kitchen. Anyway it was worth more than £90 million in mouse money. When I opened the door they hardly had time to say hello, much less to come out. They were really mad with joy. They thought their kitchen cabinet far finer than Tatania's Palace, the doll's house which had taken forty years to make and which had recently been sold at Sotheby's for £130,000; and which had tiny copies of *The Times* on the tables and miniature Gainsboroughs on the walls.

Tracey and Keith had put a touch of magic into our lives as well as those of the little mice. We felt stronger again now. Nothing could ever be so bad again. Was it chance? Was it fate?

Perhaps relations not of flesh and blood are closest. Tracey was born on 2nd October like me. We were sister Libras. We could fit on the same wavelength and in the same clothes. It was like magic. I felt a strange love for her. There are about five people in the world whose minds I admire and who are special to me. Tracey became the sixth and the only one a woman. Could we have been lovers in some past life, or sisters in some future?

We arrived back in the caravan after the Christmas holiday to find that furry visitors in from the cold wind had devoured *Woman's Own* more thoroughly than any waiting dental patient. But loyally they had only nibbled around the very edges of our glossy photograph in the main feature.

Colin's same striped shirt which he had arrived back in Plymouth in so long ago hung up in the caravan. It was now his only shirt, as it had been then. The ghosts of the fine attire of in between were fading. The striped shirt had changed strangely little since we arrived back after our round the world voyage – but we had ...

Libras don't mind poverty; don't mind hardship. But they can't bear squalor. I have slept by the roadside in damp ditches, among long itchy grasses, in forests. But leaves and trees are never sordid, as this mildewy tiny caravan now seemed, with its two rings that heated endless gruel when we could afford gas. The children were happy and well and laughter seeped into the unlovely walls. But for how long? Really, I felt they had been in less danger in our small clean boat among the wild open waves.

All this cycled round my mind and I thought again of the letter tucked in a mouse's hole in a corner. I had half hoped they would eat it, but they hadn't. I had always hidden letters if they came inviting only me to do things. Financial peace came second to family peace. Colin always said that if we were to survive as a 'family unit' we should only do performances together, as a family. I had always agreed with this in principle. But I had been sad at the interesting things I'd had to give up. In bad moods I fumed that it was all right for me to risk my life and go off to get sponsorship alone, etc, etc.

BBC South-West now wanted me on a discussion programme, to choose a topical subject to talk about for half an hour...

I thought back, to 'The Marje Proops Programme' and to the BBC2 'Book Programme' when I had been torn between my love for my book which was like a child and love for my husband. We'd gone to the studio, it was to be a live Robert Robinson programme. It was billed in the *Radio Times*, but five minutes before it started we had left in a storm of producers and production assistants. Because I'd written the books they'd only wanted me and Colin had insisted that we do nothing if we didn't do it together. I now shuddered at how rude I'd been to the studio.

Surely in a real family it shouldn't matter who earns the money, because a real family is one. But Colin had smashed my typewriters, thrown coffee all over the dust-covers of my books. When photographers came I often had to move quickly beside him, because if he wasn't in the picture too, family life would be most stormy for the next few days. Colin deserved all the great deal of recognition he got. Why was he so mean to me, while publicly telling everyone how proud of my writing he was? Why did he want more? I didn't blame him, but when he ranted and raved at trival things, and spoilt the hard, shakily-won rewards of achievement, it nibbled away at the magic of our life together.

The burden was intolerable. Both Colin and I took to going regularly to see Tracey and Keith and felt better again. One day I went up to see the bulldogs and somehow with the second cup of coffee I did what I'd never done to a living soul before. I discussed my problem with Tracey and the burden lifted. For I felt she was part of me. How could I be betraying Colin by telling part of myself about him? She was so wise. I often wondered about Tracey. She was one of the most elegant and feminine women I had ever met. But also the most strong. I wondered where her secret strength came from.

I had struggled as hard to keep my marriage afloat and sailing as ever I had *Anneliese* in the Southern Ocean; and it had been much more difficult. I kept silent and smiled and tried not to give up, for my children as well as Colin and my life were on board. I'd often felt I was the wrong sort of wife for him anyway; too strong-willed and independent.

Now I looked again at that letter inviting me to go to Plymouth and was determined to go this time. Doing things alone might damage the family. Well, starving would damage the family too. And the £60 fee would mean a lot just now. I looked at Eve's and Jimmy's worn plimsolls and felt a surge of pleasure at the new shoes I would be able to afford for them.

How many hollow-eyed mornings had come after nights writing while the rest of the family's snores provided the background music to the typewriter. And when the books were published, Colin often only shouted crossly. Many people were kind about them and anyway maybe work is its own reward, and Colin often very sweetly looked after the children while I was writing. But afterwards the gold of a 'well done' from the person I loved most was seldom there. I so longed for it.

I rang the producer and told him I had decided to talk about bad news, scandal, junk food for the eyes. Two hundred miles offshore from Plymouth at the end of our last voyage, we had turned on the radio for the first time and listened to the news. We had hardly dared come back. But when we eventually sailed into Plymouth Hoe we'd found that the sun was still shining, the birds were singing and people didn't look too hungry. Why was a businessman's scandal worth fat headlines on the front page while a news item telling how six million pounds had been gathered to save whales from extinction was relegated to half an inch on the fourth page.

Probably if at the time the newspapers had been less full of the King's abdication so that he could marry Mrs Simpson, they would have had more room for the real problems in Europe and maybe the Second World War wouldn't have happened. People like scandal. Children like chocolate. But do you give it to them for breakfast?

I worked on this and two weeks later set off for Plymouth in my old jeans and leaky shoes. But there was a magic bag under my arm. And by the time I got to the studio I was dressed in one of Tracey's pretty lace bras which fitted me, frilly Janet Reger knickers, tights and a beautiful pink trousersuit of hers. Perhaps Cinderella had had a little orange bag under her arm as well!

The pink suit did well. Next morning the local paper took its picture and people came up and told me they'd liked what I'd said. One dear old lady undid a half pound of butter ... which she'd just bought, for me to do my autograph in. The presents I was able to bring back for the family were more than magic and the light in the children's eyes lit the frame of our fortune again.

Then one day what seemed like a miracle happened. A sheaf of time cards arrived to count the change of time down to the last second farthing. A little later one solitary member of Fibreglass Bill's team arrived back on board and started laminating. Something had been settled between Granary and Fibreglass Bill and we were creeping towards financial Cape Horn again.

The days of January came and went. Work proceeded slowly. Granary kept silent. Had the financial hurricane calmed, or were we in the eye of it? Tracey and Keith kept us cheerful and filled our bodies with five-star fuel many times each week.

Early one wet morning I had a personal tragedy. My old rusty bicycle, my stoic friend through many miles almost as dear to me as my daughter, was stolen from outside the bulldogs' residence. The heavy breathing of other people's sleep leant on the air as I left the house. Mud poured in through the tops of my yachting shoes and squeezed out again through the holes in the toes in a soggy cycle as I walked desolately down to the frozen caravan to start my early morning writing.

Two hours later the caravan door opened and Tracey and Keith, shoving away the book-thoughts which filled the tiny caravan, sat down on the sofa. Tracey was holding a brown paper bag. She smiled her best cordon bleu smile and held it out. 'This is for you,' she said.

How kind, I thought, to bring sandwiches. But it was a brand new pair of the most luxurious yachting shoes I had ever seen.

'We thought you would need new shoes,' she said, 'now you have to walk.'

They must have thought me aloof and ungrateful. I could hardly thank them, in case I cried. These were more than just shoes. They were more than the thousands of pounds' worth of equipment which over the months had arrived for the boat. Somebody cared. I felt in a strange way loved. My heartstrings, still and dusty for so long, were pulled till they hurt, because it was so hard to express what I felt.

Everything seemed brighter in the days that followed. The stanchions were now appearing all round the boat. The dorsal strut to the front beam had been laminated in. The pads of foam we thought useless, but which the surveyor had insisted on, were almost in place; the holes for the chainplates had appeared and several cleats and the largest of our gorgeous three-speed Lewmar winches sprouted on deck.

Bill believed that the secret of a strong structure was in gradual change of section, like a tree's branches, and the shipwrights became busy constructing a great piece of wood to put beneath the baseplate of the mainmast to spread the load.

Our friends the bulldog pups were quite large now. Magic nature had invisibly added extra sturdy inches, and painted their noses black. How quietly and brilliantly nature worked, without any fuss or finance or board meetings or overtime.

Mantru Diamond Lil celebrated Colin's birthday on 4th February by getting married again, to Mr Frosty. The spirits looking over our shoulders still seemed to link us with those bulldogs and their human friends. Princess Tracey had to act as bridesmaid, so Colin had to make do with a giant tube of Toblerone and a gorgeous red sweater from Keith, instead of the cake she and Eve had planned together.

But the finest birthday gift for him and unbirthday present for me was the very first glimpse of our enormous beautiful silver mast at Proctors. Four sails were also ready. Surely, surely the battle was nearly over? Surely we'd get her finished now?

It was 63 days later – nearly time for the finest results of Colin's birthday. The cake that could have been baked instead would have been very stale by now. Shadows under mascara; pale under Lauder. Tracey's face had the same look my face often had when I was up at nights writing or sailing. It was nearly time for Mantru Diamond Lil to have more puppies!

All this turmoil, worry and work every six months. Why did she do it? Why did I do it? Was it the same force? The same Cape Horn spirit?

'Please, Lilly, please give me a Cruft's champion,' was Tracey's prayer to her dog as she'd sat up with her four nights. The fifth or 63rd night was B night. New clean Page Three girls now lined the sterilized playpen of the first puppies we'd met. Soon there would be another generation of bulldog pups to bound into our sleeping bag each morning when we stayed at West Road.

At midnight Keith went up to bed and Tracey and I stole the cushions away from the living room chairs and lay down with them on top of the Page Three girls in the maternity hospital, keeping a real 'dog watch' this time. Several times I woke up feeling deaf and found that the fat Lil had one front paw in my ear, the other on Tracey's head.

For the sake of the same harmony I strived for with Colin, Tracey didn't argue with Keith when he said to wait till early afternoon to call the vet. But by midday still nothing had happened and she couldn't bear it any longer. Her woman's intuition went into overdrive and she rang the vet, and he came round immediately.

'She'll have to have a caesarean at once,' he said gravely. 'Bring her in.'

Oh no. It wasn't going to be as easy as Jimmy's birth. We waited in the shiny empty surgery waiting room. Each second was as heavy as an hour.

'It'll be one big dead one,' muttered Keith.

'No – there'll be ten beautiful puppies,' said Tracey. She cared more. But she had the extra courage it takes to stand on the hill and make fact climb up to one's dreams.

Tracey and I nearly fell into the reception kiosk as we leant forward and crammed our ears for sounds. All we could hear was Lil's heavy breathing coming from somewhere nearby. Then there was a high-pitched new-born squeak. The vet came in looking tired and red-eyed.

'She had a hard job,' he said. 'A little later and we'd have lost her.'

My heart almost stopped. Then a nurse followed with a basket. There they were. Five gorgeous little white princesses and one brindle. They were so beautiful. It was all worth it.

Then Lilly was wheeled in, still sleeping like a great fat Sultana. She'd be so happy when she woke up. She loved puppies so much. The nurse filled the hot-water bottle and Tracey slid it under the covers of the box we'd brought to carry the pups home in.

'You pick them up and put them in the box,' Tracey said to me, smiling.

It was like a precious gift. I marvelled as I gently picked them up one by one. My hands were sticky with the womb dampness still on their coats and I felt a great love for them and grateful to Colin too for having allowed me time away from the work and worry of the boat to witness this miracle. After all, he had helped Jimmy be born.

The puppies were so tiny. That they would eventually turn into great fat Sultanas like Lil made the pumpkin turning into a coach seem just a small miracle by comparison. I felt strange and a bit different as I crept back to the mud and the boat that evening. The shadows under my eyes would be gone by morning. But the mark on my mind of sleeping alongside Tracey and the fat Mantru Diamond Lil and seeing the brand new lives of the little puppies would stay forever.

The boat was moving ahead each day now, powered not by wind, but by the power of the chisels that drove her towards completion. Why didn't I feel happier? My fingers shook as I tried to strike the right keys on the typewriter and I jumped every time there was a knock on the door.

Then came one softer than the rest. It was a boat agent. 'I've been sent to inspect the boat and put it on the market,' he said cheerfully. 'Granary are finishing the boat so that they can sell it.'

I felt sick. The smile decayed on my face. My hands fell deadened on the keys of the typewriter. All the letters bunched cowering at the heart of it. Was this going to be the end of it all? Surely, surely not. Surely Roger wouldn't let them. We tried to get in touch with him but as usual he was travelling. He was one of us, a sailor. I was too shaken to do more than nod numbly as the agent left.

The building was now going on day by day. But the sound of the chisels was different to our ears now; the ring of the hammer an octave lower. Black depression that would have been fatal when we were sailing around Cape Horn burst through us. We had to overcome it. At sea you have to keep cheerful and calm enough to cope and help a boat survive. It was the same now. Whatever the future, we had to help the catamaran over the most critical part of her building. She depended on us just as later we would depend on her. If we acted cheerfully everything would come right.

The loudest howls of trouble couldn't distract from the drama of what was happening on board. It couldn't spoil the feeling of awe we felt as we walked about the decks. The solid stainless steel chainplates were brought on board at last. They were so strong and gleamingly beautiful that we felt sorry they were to be on the inside of the hulls where we couldn't continually admire them. The massive stress-bearing baseplate for the mast had been laminated. Pulpits had been curved round the front beam, mysterious fastenings were appearing. More gleaming winches sprouted on deck. The huge mast track was secure. Colin, worrying about how to stop the bolts from leaking, was reassured by a shipwright, 'That's all right – I'll put lots of goodness in.'

We were struggling closer and closer towards the sailing trials. When Roger saw how beautiful she was, I felt he would fight hard against any decision of his board to part with her. She was going to be a beautiful princess boat. And our real job as sailors, we were sure, was going to begin again soon. We tried not to feel too alarmed by the fact that to start with, in spite of all our plans, she would have only four sails and no engines.

Now we stood on the lovely decks and dreamed of the time we'd first sheet the great mainsail in, and see it fill with wind. We were just beginning to be able to look through the chrysalis and see the beautiful butterfly emerging. Everything on the boat was so huge. We felt we must be looking at it through a magnifying glass, or else that we had eaten some of Alice's medicine and ourselves grown smaller.

Meanwhile winter kept her promise to nature and berthed at Willment's Shipyard. The taps in the yard all froze. I was no longer able to go for my nightly wash under the fire hydrant, and in the mornings you could see the tiny footprints in the carpet snow of the children of the wild mice, unpaying guests. They also chewed around the manuscript of my latest book and I thought it was about time I sent *Libras Don't Say No* away to the publishers.

Even the seat of our rusty bicycle was soft white for the first time in its life. And after one wild night snow had sneaked Houdini-style beneath our scaffolding shed and had blown sideways into every nook and cranny on the boat. Disembarking the stowaway white crew was hours of hard work.

The thaw was even more alarming. It fattened the spring tide and the boat disappeared right up into the attic of her shed. She seemed restless and longing to be out. What would she think about the monster voyage we planned? It had been *Anneliese*'s decision to go on the last voyage. It would be her big sister's decision to go on this one. We'd ask her at the sailing trials.

We decided it was time we now started thinking of how best to sail the boat, and stopped worrying about financing her. Colin said he felt a bit like he had when coming back from the last voyage and tying up to the visitor's buoy outside the Royal Western Yacht Club in Plymouth. The chain underneath might be rusty! But there was a time when you *had* to stop worrying.

Granary were probably just showing normal battle strain and tension. For a man who had confessed that if he had been us, he'd have given up long ago, Roger Fuller had already been splendid. With his foresight and courage when things had been really low, he had saved the boat.

Early next week, little Jimmy, now six years old, deserted his girlfriend Princess Tracey in mid-walk and climbed on board the 70-foot monster after she'd been blown forward against the front of the shed in a gale. Singlehandedly seizing the handle of the biggest gleaming three-speed winch, *he winched her back three inches*!

With a strange feeling in our throats we realized that it was the first time the catamaran had ever moved under her own power. Tracey and Felcign Gervais looked on with wise eyes, sharing this moment and becoming part of the boat's future.

TWENTY-SIX

Rivers of my mind begin to part

The silence was louder than the children's laughter. We were paying a high price for the boat. It was not in any currency a bank would understand. But it was too high. It must be the last instalment; the last time.

I knew Eve and Jimmy would be all right with Keith and Tracey. They had just left on their way to stay a week with them in Southampton while the boat was here in the Isle of Wight being rigged at Spencer's, the famous riggers. At least when it was rigged it could be launched and sailed!

But I couldn't bear it. I leapt off the boat and ran down the narrow streets of Cowes, trying not to trip over sleepy labradors and docksiders on the way.

The hybrid vessel was just flexing its engines. They were just getting on board. Jimmy was all excited. He had sailed twice around the world before he was four. But this was the first time he'd been on board a hydrofoil. The look on Tracey's face made me feel happier. Eve and Jimmy were safe in the power beyond the horizon of our minds.

Cowes was like fairyland after our shipyard at Southampton. Instead of the eternal mud and aching, rusted limbs of ancient ships, there were little hills like fossilized waves on which sailed picturesque houses with oilskins in the windows, and the water of the Medina sparkled pure and clean against the expensive antifouling of the fine yachts which sailed up and down all day.

The catamaran couldn't believe her good fortune. She lay like a naked princess by the jettyside waiting to be bedecked. We spent seven magic days at Spencer's. Long silver streams of rigging went up and the beautiful silver masts were stepped. The mainmast had Jimmy's tooth under it in a place the fairies would never get to.

The mice still lived in their Tatania's Palace in the cabin, but Jackson, a baby jackdaw which had been rescued from a shipyard moggy by one of our painters, was in charge. He strutted around, picking up nails and screws and any bright thing. In the mornings he would watch me carefully and at my first stretch he would start asking for his breakfast of Granary bread and prime ham. If I didn't pay any attention he would hop over and pull my hair.

On the fifth day we lost one of the halyards up the mast and Colin lost his temper too and yelled and shouted in a way which I understood, but the magic didn't and became frayed, as I hoped our ropes would never be. That night Jackson the jackdaw hopped off with my wedding ring.

The early morning hovercraft on the seventh day was hovering less lightly than usual, as it reached the Medina. Small wonder, for Jimmy, Eve, Keith, Tracey and what seemed like a hundred food hampers were among its insides. It was time for the catamaran's first voyage.

The stringers had been undone, we'd said goodbye to all those kind people at Spencer's. Everything had been loaded on board and it looked as though we were going away for a month's voyage instead of just back to Willment's Shipyard.

We slipped away to catch the tide and get in at the other end. The big boat slewed through the water with scarcely a footprint left behind. The gentle force 2 waves welcomed the new hulls. The ghosts of little *Anneliese*'s first voyage smiled.

We had just entered Southampton Water itself when a Vosper Thornycroft frigate roared past. The wash went wild. Yachts rolled like horses in the morning. But our boat, wise to her heritage, to her godfather Cape Horn, sat lightly on the water. The champagne scarcely quivered in the plastic cups. Tracey bent forward and spilt some over the bows for the boat to taste. Colin took another swig and laughed. The last time we'd done this ceremony had been on board little *Anneliese* at Cape Horn itself, 9,512 miles from home.

Now the pilot boats, the tugboats, tooted their sirens and saluted the monster catamaran's first voyage. People on the ferryboats waved. The river police stood on the foredeck of their fast launch and cheered. The only silent vessels were the morose giant tankers with their ugly bulbous bows moored near Fawley. Our boat sailed faster now than many motorboats. But she was in the hands of the four elements. She was a free boat who would be lucky because she didn't harm the world.

There we were on board, drinking champagne and eating turkey. My two beautiful children all blond and rosy cheered, jumped and played on the foredeck with Tracey and Gervais and their laughter was louder than the sirens themselves.

Suddenly there was a shout from astern. It was two *Anneliese*s come up to greet their big sister. One had Bill O'Brien on board, his friendly Irish face smiling from ear to ear. He looked so proud. There was the same pipe in his mouth as when he'd first stood at the end of the muddy jetty and instructed us how to put up the sails on *Anneliese* while she was still safely grounded on the low-tide mud berth. That was so many sea centuries ago.

I thought of all our struggles and tears and hardships that lay behind this moment: that journey to the Persian Gulf; our last 12p for the milkman; the clover round the tiny tent we'd had to survive in. We were approaching the great new bridge that spans the Itchen. Passing under it was the startline of the boat's life.

The great silver mainmast stretched up to the sky like a magic wand. Both the sun and the moon, our faithful ocean guides, looked on together and cheered in the clear sky. The sun kissed the masts with a million blinding reflections. The moon was gentler but she had come out specially and her presence meant more than all the sirens.

It seemed impossible we'd ever get under the bridge. The harbour master had promised two feet to spare. As we aimed exactly for the centre span, we hoped he was right. I looked up and held my breath and all the bridges of my life seemed to flash before me. New Bridge of my childhood where the old man had taken my knickers off. Sydney Harbour Bridge at the start of our voyage to Cape Horn. Severn Bridge where we'd had our muesli picnic off our orange plastic plates. The bridge at Strasbourg where I'd slept beside the poor frozen dead bird ...

The mice were running their wheel trying to help, their tails curled up in fun. Jackson sat snoozing, balanced on one leg and with just one beady black eye open on watch. The hamster lay asleep in a fragrance of cabbage larder mattress. Outside Felcign Gervais stretched his beautiful boxer body and gazed at me with wise eyes, and the children, sea children again, back to their heritage, sat with Princess Tracey on the foredeck.

It was the first time we had ever sailed with more than just ourselves on board. It felt funny having other people on our catamaran. But they were family too now. They had shared a moment we had dreamed about for four years. They had shared an experience with us, more intimate than lovemaking on a honeymoon.

Then the two men started arguing in this moment of triumph. Their loud harsh voices vibrated against the beautiful hulls. And I couldn't stand it. In the middle of our happiness I reached breaking-point. I thought despairingly of the task of soothing these two down ... Why should I do it?

Something strange was happening between Colin and me. It was sad. You can lie to others. But you cannot lie to your own brain. Our streams which had run together for so long were dividing. Perhaps they would run down different sides of the mountain. I looked at his face and hoped that he would be happy. Jackson already knew what was happening when he had hopped off with my wedding ring.

I looked at Tracey and at the ten thousand stories on her face. I felt a surge of power between us. I knew the boat loved her. There was Colin, bad-tempered and vulnerable, but my partner for so long: and Tracey, my partner for much longer, but unknown and invisible through the centuries.

She was a woman and I had never felt even particularly friendly to any woman before. What was happening now? And why? The same clothes fitted each of our bodies. The same thoughts each of our minds. Our talk was mental lovemaking. But we didn't really need to say much for if you are on the same wavelength the signals don't have to be very loud.

What did destiny want of us? I felt there was something special we had to do together. Perhaps a voyage. Perhaps an experience.

The feeling I had for her was so beautiful it could not be wrong. It was extraordinary, for I had always loved men and the company of men. My tits had embarrassed me by filling the newspapers. I'd always disliked being with women and in my childhood had dreaded the drooping bosoms of female relations kissing me goodnight.

I hardly dared to think about the way I felt towards Tracey in case it disappeared. I'd never tell Tracey I loved her, but I did, and the feeling was more moral than going to bed with my husband Colin after a row.

I read somewhere that there is only about one per cent difference between men and women. The blinkers that state you can only truly love someone of the opposite sex say that what goes on below the waist rules the mind. But male and female minds are similar enough to do the same exams. Now I felt a pure love for Tracey, crystal and delicate, yet so powerful that it touched the whole of me, every thought, all the time.

There was poor cross Colin, the Champion Insulter, the past shadowing his mind. There was the beautiful, triumphant boat. And the beautiful frolicking children laughing with Tracey. What a strange turn life had taken. What did the fates hold in store for us?